The World's WORST DISASTERS of the TWENTIETH CENTURY

The World's
WORST
DISASTERS
of the
TWENTIETH
CENTURY

Exeter Books

NEW YORK

First published in USA 1984
by Exeter Books
Distributed by Bookthrift
Exeter is a trademark of Simon & Schuster, Inc.
Bookthrift is a registered trademark of Simon & Schuster, Inc.
New York, New York

ISBN 0 671 31238 3

Made and printed in Great Britain by
Richard Clay (The Chaucer Press) Limited
Bungay, Suffolk

Acknowledgements

The publishers would like to thank the following organisations and individuals for their kind permission to reproduce the photographs in this book:

Irish Times 171, Keystone Press Agency 2 below, 25 inset, 34, 42, 62–3, 69, 72, 75, 78, 83, 84, 90, 97, 156, Popperfoto 2 middle right, 46, 115, 116, 121, 129, 132, 136, 151, Press Association 109, Radio Times Hulton Picture Library 49, Topham 2 above, middle left, 10, 11, 17, 19, 22, 23, 25, 30, Wide World Photos 142, 158, 176, 178–9. News Ltd 188–9.

Contents

The Mont Pelèe Volcano (1902)   8

San Francisco Earthquake (1906)   14

The Titanic (1912)   21

Tokyo Earthquake (1923)   28

The R 101 (1930) and the Hindenberg (1937)   34

The Morro Castle (1934)   44

Naples Black Market Express (1944)   51

The London Pea-Soupers (1952)   56

Le Mans (1955)   60

Agadir Earthquake (1960)   67

The Vaiont Dam (1963)   74

The Florence Floods (1966)   81

Astronauts (1976) and Cosmonauts (1971)   88

Peru Earthquake (1970)   95

Mass Poisoning in Iraq (1971-1972)   102

Isle of Man Summerland Fire (1973)   106

Ermenonville Forest Air Crash (1974)   113

American Mid-West Tornadoes (1974)   119

The Honduras Hurricane (1974)   124

Seveso Chemical Disaster (1976)   128

The Tenerife Plane Crash (1977)   135

The Big Heat (1980)   140

North Sea Oil Rig Disaster (1980)   145

The Las Vegas MGM Fire (1980)   155

Mount St Helen's Eruption (1980)   162

St Valentine's Day Fire (1981)   169

The Potomac River Airliner Crash (1982)   174

The Australian Bush Fires (1983)   186

The Mont Pelée Volcano (1902)

It may not be good for the tourist trade to call some of the Lesser Antilles the Volcanic Caribees, but that is what they are. Stretching in an arc from the Virgin Islands in the north to Grenada in the south, the Windward and the Leeward Islands have been built up from the ocean floor by volcanic action. On some the volcanoes are extinct, on others, still active. Only two have erupted in historic times, Mont Pelée on Martinique and La Soufrière on St Vincent.

Martinique is now a Department of France, so firmly integrated that when someone says '*Je vais en métropole*' he means he is going to Paris, not Fort de France, the island's capital. But in 1902 the most important commercial centre was St Pierre, a town of 26,000 inhabitants, lying in a mile-long, crescent-shaped strip on the north-west coast, below ravines rising steeply towards Mont Pelée ('bald mountain') which reared, 4,430 feet above sea level, five miles away, almost due north.

Sugar, rum and bananas were the basis of the island's prosperity. St Pierre was a gay town – people called it the Paris of the West Indies – with riotous tropical vegetation, a mixed population of whites, mulattos and blacks, and strongly contrasting wealth and poverty.

Mont Pelée steamed and puffed occasionally, rather like an old man smoking his pipe. The main crater had remained dormant for ages, although there had been a minor eruption in the volcano 50 years earlier. For as long as anyone could remember there had been a lake there called *L'Etang des Palmistes*, and it was a favourite picnic spot. The only other eruption recorded had been in 1792 and that, too, had been insignificant.

On the south side of the mountain, facing St Pierre, there was a dry secondary crater, *L'Etang Sec,* with steep flanks unbroken except at one point, where, also on the south side, a gash in the rim led into a ravine called *La Rivière Blanche* which extended right to the coast. In the rainy season flood water flowing down this and other ravines could cause considerable damage.

On 2 April 1902, fresh steaming vent-holes were noticed in the upper part of *La Rivière Blanche*. Three weeks later, a small amount of volcanic ash floated down on to the streets of St Pierre and there were a few earth tremors, just enough to upset crockery. In the following days the situation became more ominous. There were explosions in the secondary crater which hurled up rocks and clouds of ash. Then a lake formed there, 200 yards across, and also a cinder cone as high as a house, with steam spurting from the top. Soon ash was falling more heavily, mantling and muffling the town, seeping into shops and houses, killing birds and animals and bringing with it the nauseating stench of sulphur. Mrs Prentiss, wife of the American consul, wrote: 'The smell is so strong that horses in the street stop and snort, and some of them drop dead in their harness.'

In response to the considerable alarm caused by these events, Louis Mouttet, Governor of Martinique, appointed a commission to assess the situation and he visited the town. It was the last trip he ever made. Incredibly, the commission reported no immediate danger and while Mouttet maintained a studied air of calm the local newspaper, *Les Colonies*, backed him up with soothing editorials. The extraordinary complacency of all three has been ascribed to political collusion: important elections were due to be held on 10 May and Mouttet was anxious not to let his supporters disperse.

As ash continued to fall, St Pierre began to look like a body drained of blood. Deep rumblings could be heard coming from the belly of the mountain. Despite troops brought in by the Governor, law and order became difficult to maintain. Shops and businesses closed. Terrified villagers from the mountain slopes burst into bars and hotels demanding refuge. From the other end of the town, people were pouring southwards, swelling the population of St Pierre to 30,000. On 5 May came a foretaste of what Pelée could do. The cleft in its side becoming blocked with ash, massive quantities of rain water had collected in *L'Etang Sec*, been heated by volcanic action and now burst out in a seething torrent of boiling mud to hurtle down the mountain side. The tide engulfed a sugar-mill on the coast north of St Pierre, killing over 100 people, then plunged into the sea, causing a huge wave which swamped the lower parts of the town. *Les Colonies* reported 'the entire city afoot' and 'a flood of humanity pouring up from the low point of the anchorage, not knowing where to turn.'

Far worse was to come. On 6 May Pelée's rumblings turned to a steady roar interspersed with explosions which threw up masses of red-hot cinders. And the Governor did something unforgivable: he stationed troops on the roads to stop people leaving the town. *Les Colonies* found a disreputable professor to declare: 'Mont Pelée is no more to be feared than Vesuvius is feared by Naples. Where could one be better off than in St Pierre?' In a proclamation the Mayor gave his support: 'Please allow us to advise you to return to your normal occupations.'

All through Wednesday 7 May the roaring and the explosions continued.

THE MONT PELÉE VOLCANO

View of St Pierre

Heavy rain sent more torrents of mud down the mountain carrying huge boulders many tons in weight. Mingled with water, the ash gave the town a top-coating of hot sticky paste. There was only one slender ray of hope for the 30,000 residents: La Soufrière on St Vincent was reported to be in eruption. Perhaps that would relieve the pressure.

Thursday dawned clear and sunny. The people glanced apprehensively upwards to Pelée, and were relieved to see only a vapour column of unusual height. At 6.30 a.m. a passenger ship, the S.S. *Roraima*, arrived in port and tied up alongside 17 other vessels. By then the scene was dramatically different. 'For hours before we entered the roadstead,' said Assistant Purser Thompson, 'we could see flames and smoke rising from Mont Pelée. No one on board had any idea of danger. As we approached we could distinguish the rolling and leaping red flames that belched from the mountain in huge volume and gushed high in the sky. Enormous clouds of black smoke hung over the volcano. The flames were then spurting straight up in the air, now and then waving to one side or the other a moment, and again suddenly leaping higher up. There was a constant muffled roar. It was like the biggest oil refinery in the world burning up on the mountain top.'

Thompson thought the spectacle magnificent. Almost everyone on board was watching. There were no premonitions, except perhaps on the part of the Captain, who told a passenger: 'I am not going to stay any longer than I can help.'

But he stayed too long. The mountain-side facing the town was already glowing red-hot and at 7.52 a.m. exactly (the time was recorded on the military hospital clock which somehow escaped destruction) it exploded. 'There was no warning,' wrote Thompson. 'The side of the volcano was ripped out and there hurled towards us a solid wall of flame. It sounded like a thousand cannons. The wave of fire was on us and over us like a lightning flash, a hurricane of fire which rolled in mass straight down on St Pierre and the shipping. The town vanished before our eyes . . .'

In fact there were two explosions, one which shot upwards from the main crater in a dense black cloud pierced with lightning flashes and the other which blew out sideways from *L'Etang Sec*. Expanding sulphurous gases had shattered lava into fragments and now, through the gaping cleft in the secondary crater, a murderous avalanche of white-hot particles mixed with gas and superheated steam tore down *La Rivière Blanche* at hurricane speed.

From its effect on metals it has been calculated that the temperature of the blast was around 1,000°C. People died almost instantaneously wherever they happened to be, with hardly a struggle or a movement, from the inhalation of the fiery gases or from burns, some stripped of all clothing by

Mont Pelée

the blast. Of the entire population of 30,000 only two men survived. Thompson recalled: 'After the explosion not one living being was seen on land.' The town was reduced to a heap of smoking rubble. Walls were torn down, metal roofs ripped off and crumpled like paper, trees stripped to the bare trunks. Within seconds, as the blast passed over, St Pierre reappeared as an ancient ruin, stripped of every mark that had given it identity, like something from pre-history unearthed by archaeologists, though here no digging was necessary. There was no lava crust as at Pompeii, only ash. Searching the ruins later, rescue workers could barely recognize even well-known streets.

The situation in the harbour was little better. The *nuée ardente*, or 'glowing cloud' had caused a tidal wave which capsized or badly damaged every ship, and only one managed to escape to St Lucia with 22 of her crew dead or severely burned. 'Wherever the fire struck the sea,' said Thompson, 'the water boiled and sent up great clouds of steam. The blast shrivelled and set fire to everything it touched. Only 25 of those on the *Roraima* out of 68 were left after the first flash. The fire swept off the ship's masts and smoke-stack as if they had been cut by a knife.'

Thompson saved his life by burying himself under bedding in his cabin. The *Roraima* was in no state to put to sea. One passenger who survived, a Barbadian nurse, described how ash poured in through a skylight in 'boiling splashes' as she and their mother were dressing three children for breakfast. The cabin was filling up with the scalding stuff when the first engineer heard their screams and helped them to the forward deck. By then one little boy was dead and a baby was dying. Parts of the ship were on fire and now the whole town was 'one mass of roaring flames'. 'My mistress lay on the deck in a collapsed state. The lady was collected and resigned, handed me some money, told me to take Rita (the surviving child) to her aunt, and sucked a piece of ice before she died.' On the other ships the boiling ash stuck to men's clothing, coating them from head to foot and baking them alive. Some were seen crawling about the decks, charred beyond recognition. Many jumped overboard and 'their scorched flesh sizzled as it entered the water.'

One of the two survivors in St Pierre was a Negro shoemaker, Léon Compère-Léandre, aged 28. He was sitting on his doorstep when disaster struck. 'All of a sudden I felt a terrible wind blowing, the earth began to tremble and the sky suddenly became dark. I turned to go into the house, made with great difficulty the three or four steps that separated me from my room, and felt my arms and legs burning, also my body. I collapsed over a table.' Others came into the room, 'crying and writhing with pain, although their clothes showed no sign of having been touched by flame.' Very soon all were dead, also an old man that Léandre found in the house. 'He was purple and inflated, but the clothing was intact. . . . Crazed and almost overcome, I threw myself on a bed, inert and awaiting death. My senses returned to me in perhaps an hour, when I saw that the roof was on fire.' Léandre owed his life to an incredible fluke. Out of all those people, for reasons which will never be known, his lungs escaped fatal damage.

The other survivor was Auguste Ciparis, a 25-year-old Negro stevedore, who was due to be hanged for murder. He was lodged in a structure almost certainly unique in the entire town, a condemned cell, reminiscent of the modern Nissen hut, in the shape of a bisected circle, resting against the outer wall of the local prison. At the front was an aperture blocked by a solid door so low that it could only be entered on all-fours. Above it was a small, heavily grated window. Massively constructed to prevent prisoners getting out, the cell protected Ciparis from the full blast.

Dressed in shirt, trousers and hat, he was waiting for his breakfast when the window suddenly darkened and he was struck by searing heat. At the same moment there was a resounding crash as the prison wall collapsed on the roof. Then, as ash blocked out the window entirely, Ciparis found himself in total darkness. 'I smelled nothing but my own body burning,' he said later. 'Soon I heard nothing but my own unanswered cries for help.'

Three days later, when the town could be entered by rescuers, Ciparis was released, horribly burnt but coherent. He was reprived, with a suspended sentence, and lived until 1929, earning a living as a side-show attraction in a circus: the Prisoner of St Pierre, complete with a replica of his cell.

On 20 May 1902, another eruption of Pelée combined with an earthquake drove many people from Martinique for ever: 2,000 were killed and several villages destroyed. More violent eruptions occurred on 26 May, 6 June, 9 July, and 30 August. There was a pause until September 1929, when once again the terrible *nuée ardente* roared down, with its super-heated steam, gases and incandescent particles, and tore up the modest structures of a new town which 1,000 intrepid citizens had struggled to build. This time Pelée was too late to catch a living soul: the inhabitants had read the signs and had gone. And this time no Governor tried to stop them.

San Francisco Earthquake (1906)

The sounds preceding an earthquake can be as terrifying as the event itself, particularly when they come to the ears of people dazed with sleep. Sometimes there is a boom like distant gunfire, or a sharp, snapping sound. There may be a rumbling noise like heavy traffic moving over cobbled streets. As they move forward, shock waves oscillate with a pull-and-push motion while others called 'strike waves' mingle with them, throwing off impulses at right angles. The total effect is like a clod of earth being shaken in a sieve.

The citizens of San Francisco heard a low and ominous rumble at twelve and a half minutes past five o'clock on the morning of Wednesday, 18 April 1906. A few seconds later came the first shock. William James (brother of novelist Henry James), was in a hotel bedroom with his wife. As the furniture began to rock and dance he stayed remarkably calm. 'This is an earthquake', he said to his trembling spouse, 'there is no cause for alarm' – and proceeded to dress with careful deliberation. The whole hotel now seemed to be bumping about.

Most of the 340,000 population were not so detached, though they had experienced lesser earthquakes before, the most recent in 1898 and 1900. This one was much more severe, more ruthless. There were three shocks, separated by only a few seconds and the third was by far the heaviest. One city official later reported watching horror-struck as a massive oak wardrobe in his bedroom tipped sideways, backwards and sideways again before being hurled forward and splintering into pieces. A local businessman wrote: 'I was awakened by a very severe shock. The shaking was so violent that it nearly threw me out of bed.' A bookcase was thrown off the wall, everything on tables and the mantelpiece was swept off as in a sudden roll at sea and the floor was littered with smashed china and glass.

Another man in a lodging-house bedroom saw chunks of plaster falling from the ceiling. Then through a gap a child's foot appeared. The next moment, the whole building gave a lurch, the gap closed under violent compression and the foot was severed in a gush of blood. At that point the man panicked and jumped through an open window, just in time to escape from the collapsing house.

A few people were out of doors when the earthquake struck. One was the editor of the *San Francisco Examiner*. He had just left his office with some of the staff and was chatting with them on a side-walk when the ground started rocking violently and they were thrown off their feet. All around, buildings were swaying and tipping under the shocks, throwing down showers of glass, bricks and masonry in a cloud of dust. Tram-lines were snapping under the pressure and reared up like thick metal snakes, short-circuiting in blinding sparks as overhead cables fell on them. Ominously the men could smell gas.

Two young men, Fred Walker and his friend Carlos, had arrived in the city that evening for a sight-seeing tour, coming by sea through the Golden Gate, the passage that links the land-locked Bay with the Pacific. (There was no bridge in those days; it was opened in 1937.) They had put up in a good-class hotel in the north-east corner of the oblong peninsula on which the city stands, not far from the area known as Chinatown, then as now the biggest Chinese settlement outside the Orient.

If the next day had not brought a different scene, the young men might have noted the city's breathtakingly beautiful setting on its hilly strip of land bounded on three sides by water, met some of its robust, independent-minded citizens, and seen one thing more which summed up San Francisco's flamboyant optimism: the $7,000,000 Palace Hotel. Enrico Caruso had arrived to sing with the Metropolitan Opera in *Carmen* and was staying there that night.

Fred and Carlos felt drawn to Chinatown. Its opium dens, gaming saloons, twisting alleys, and grubby, vicious, colourful life drew them like a magnet and they explored it for hours, until nearly 5.00 a.m.

Twelve minutes later, as they were walking back to their hotel, came the rumbling sounds, then the first shock. Fred was thrown against a wall, while buildings all around began to heave. As terrified people in their night clothes rushed screaming into the streets the two hurried on and found their hotel had become a pile of rubble with no sign of a single survivor.

While the Palace Hotel was rocking Caruso is said to have sung a few notes through an open window to make sure he had not lost his voice. Then he went out and sat on his suitcase in the street until someone took him to another hotel. There, pampered but resolute, he swore never to come back to San Francisco. He never did.

Meanwhile, the shocks had toppled some of the fine mansions and left others leaning at an angle of 15 degrees from the vertical. Most of the buildings in Market Street, bisecting the wealthy north from the poorer south part of the city, had been shaken to pieces as well as, except for its massive domed tower, the huge City Hall, only recently completed and supposed to be shock-proof. Elsewhere in the smart quarter a hotel in Valencia Street had

Capital city destroyed

An earthquake only days before Christmas virtually wiped the Nicaraguan capital of Managua off the map in 1972. The two jolts, lasting only seconds, came at 12.28 a.m. on 22 December. An eye-witness said: 'I saw dust rise like a blanket being lifted across the city. Then I saw nothing but fires.' Between 11,000 and 12,000 people died, hundreds of them hawkers sleeping under the central market building. Seventy five others died – 17 of them babies – when the city's general hospital collapsed, but doctors set up emergency operating theatres in the grounds, and asked car drivers to shine their lights as medical staff treated 5,000 casualties. All fire-fighting equipment was lost under rubble, and it was dawn before a fire-engine arrived after a six-hour race from neighbouring Costa Rica. More than 300,000 people – 75 per cent of the capital's population – were homeless by then, and refugees were already streaming out of the city. Among them was a pale, thin man who had been staying at the Intercontinental Hotel. Billionaire recluse Howard Hughes had been flushed out into the open briefly, before being whisked away in a private jet.

gently subsided like a deflating balloon, ending up with the fourth floor at ground level from which the people emerged unharmed.

The worst damage from earthquake alone was in the downtown area, near the site of the original Spanish settlement, Mission Dolores. But loss of life was comparatively small and within a couple of hours many citizens could be seen with utensils salvaged from their shattered homes cheerfully cooking breakfast in the streets. Things could have been worse, they were saying.

Then came the fire. Throughout the city, fires started in dozens of different places, in abandoned buildings from heaters left burning, from hearths, kitchen-ranges, or sparked by electricity or the ignition of gas escaping from broken mains. One housewife struck a match in what had been her kitchen and caused an explosion which ended in hundreds of houses being burned to the ground.

Months before, Fire Chief Danny Sullivan had warned city officials that his Service might be unable to cope with a serious conflagration. Now his words proved horribly true. For 52 fires there were only 38 horse-drawn fire-engines. Great fissures in the streets had fractured every single water main. Except from artesian wells here and there, or from the sea in fires close to the shore, there was not a drop of water to pour on the blaze.

Fanned and driven forward by a stiff breeze the fires were beginning to coalesce into a single inferno and a refugee described the sight from one of the city's many hills. 'Looking down we saw the great tide of fire roaring in the hollow, burning so steadily yet so fast that it had the effect of immense deliberation; roaring on towards miles of uninhabited dwellings so lately emptied of life that they appeared consciously to await their immolation.' He saw roofs and hilltops standing out starkly against the glare of the flames and 'sparks belching like the spray of bursting seas'.

By noon on that first day the fire was totally out of control. Federal troops summoned by the one telegraph wire still intact were on the way, as were units of the National Guard and 600 helpers from the University of California at Berkeley on the east side of the harbour. On the spot, amid the inferno, only two things could be attempted: to save as many lives as possible and blast a gap in the path of the flames. All that afternoon and through the red-glowing night, as the whole of Chinatown was being reduced to ashes, as well as the Palace Hotel, every house but one on Nob Hill, and thousands of houses, shacks, sheds and shanties in the rest of the city, the Navy ferried streams of refugees across the Bay to Oakland on the eastern shore while volunteers strove desperately to keep embarkation points clear of fire. For many there could be no rescue; they had been burned to death where they lay

San Francisco, devastated by the earthquake

Southern Italy devastated by earthquakes

Six violent earthquakes hit Southern Italy on 23 November 1980, killing 2,614 people, 47 of them worshippers in a church at Balvano. Further tremors hit the area, between Naples and Salerno, in the next few days, and on 26 November Interior Minister Virginio Rognoni offered his resignation after a row over 'slow action' by the government, but his offer was rejected. On 23 January 1981, the area was hit by severe blizzards, and a month later another 'quake killed eight more people.

trapped beneath the rubble of their homes. Eighty died in this way in one hotel. As the flames came closer, one man, who was trapped, persuaded a policeman to shoot him.

Attempts to create fire-breaks by dynamiting buildings failed. The explosive charges, laid by inexperienced men, were mostly too heavy, making buildings blow outwards instead of collapsing, so starting new fires. On the morning of the second day, Brigadier Funston, commanding federal troops, wired Washington: 'San Francisco practically destroyed. You cannot send too many tents and rations. 200,000 homeless.'

The fires were still raging when a tide of frantic people who had lost everything they possessed began looting. Mayor Schmitz issued a proclamation: 'The Federal Troops . . . have been authorized by me to KILL any and all persons found engaged in looting or in the commission of any other crime.' At the same time soup-kitchens were started and hordes of refugees were fed. One thing was certain: San Franciscans might die from a bullet, but once over the initial shock would never succumb to despair. Some of the accompanying photographs illustrate the resilience required of most San Franciscans.

Fringe areas of the city were saved, but by the Saturday, when the fires were at last burning themselves out, four square miles had been annihilated: 514 blocks containing 28,000 buildings, 450 people had been killed. Loss from earthquake was assessed later at £7 million; from fire no less than £140 million.

Recovery was a daunting prospect, but led by their level-headed Mayor the citizens rallied extraordinarily, helped by a flood of assistance from outside and also by their innate ruggedness and optimism. Many of them were descended from those tough individualists who had come halfway across the world to take part in the 1848 gold rush. Since then there had been many fires and several earthquakes, but every challenge had been met. Now

Many buildings which escaped the earthquake were destroyed by raging fires

this new one, great as it was, found them undaunted, their civic pride profoundly touched. Even while the fires were still raging orders were being placed for new tram-lines and other equipment. Within two days enough rail track had been repaired for trains to start taking out people whose homes were in other states. Electricity was restored in two weeks.

Proudly, or arrogantly, according to the point of view, San Francisco calls itself 'the city that knows how', but at least the title is deserved. Within three years, while thousands of the victims awaited resettlement in tented camps, more than a third of the city was rebuilt, not simply as a repetition of the old but on new plans with many buildings made earthquake- and fire-resistant. In 1911 the seal on total recovery was set when Congress approved San Francisco as the location of a world's fair to commemorate the opening of the Panama Canal. As if recovery from disaster was not enough, a 650-acre site was then reclaimed from tidal land stretching down from the Golden Gate, covered with landscaped gardens, pavilions, miniature palaces, and the Panama Pacific International Exposition was opened in February 1915. By the time it closed in December, 19,000,000 people had been through the gates.

Nine years had passed since that afternoon when the *Evening World Herald* of Omaha, Nebraska, had reported: '3.45 p.m. EXTRA. San Francisco wrecked and helpless.' Now every trace of that disaster had been obliterated, every connection except one: the cause. That crack in the earth's crust known as the San Andreas Fault had been the culprit, when movement occurred in the rocks on either side. The fault runs for 600 miles from Cape Mendocino in the north to the Colorado Desert, under the sea west of the Golden Gate and down the centre of the peninsula on which San Francisco stands. Along that whole length shifts in the land mass occur frequently, though none has been as severe as in 1906. They cannot be controlled; the most to be hoped for is that some day they will be predicted with greater accuracy. Meanwhile, San Francisco, one of the world's greatest seaports and trading centres, lives on, with its 2,000,000 inhabitants, beautiful, tough, cosmopolitan, energetic, disaster-prone – the city that has known how to survive.

The Titanic (1912)

Even at the outset, the *Titanic*'s maiden voyage was marked by near-tragedy. As the immense 46,329-ton vessel moved majestically from her berth at Southampton, she came abreast of a moored liner, the *New York*. Suddenly there came a number of loud reports as the other's thick mooring-ropes snapped like string, and then the two ships began to be drawn irresistibly together. The *Titanic* was stopped, just in time, the strange 'suction' ceased, and tugs nosed the *New York* back to her berth. An identical situation arose a few minutes later when the *Teutonic* also strained at her ropes and heeled over several degrees until the *Titanic* had slid past.

Then the liner was lifting to the surge of the open sea and her crew relaxed. High on the liner's bridge Captain Edward Smith relaxed with them. Beneath his feet, the deck trembling almost imperceptibly with the thrust of her massive turbines, was the largest, the finest and the safest ship that had ever been built. To guarantee that safety, 15 transverse bulkheads subdivided her from stem to stern; a double bottom was a further guarantee against accident. She was, in the mind of everyone ashore and afloat, the ultimate – the unsinkable ship.

After a brief call at Cherbourg, the *Titanic* left Queenstown (now Cobh) in Ireland during the evening of Thursday, 11 April 1912 and headed out into the Atlantic and waters which the veteran Captain Smith knew well. She steamed steadily westwards, without further incident; the sea was calm, the weather clear and brilliantly bright but very cold. Indeed, the temperature dropped dramatically during the morning of Sunday, 14 April and radio messages received by the *Titanic*'s Marconi man warned of the danger of icebergs.

The ship continued to race on at full speed, her lights twinkling on the dark still water, her engines thrusting her forward at a steady 22 knots. Then, just before midnight, a look-out suddenly screamed, 'Iceberg right ahead!'

Frantic orders were given which would have swung the liner's bows to port, but it was too late. As they began the swing an immense iceberg scraped along her starboard side then slipped astern into the night. Captain Smith was on the bridge almost before his First Officer Murdoch could ring 'Stop engines!' He ordered all watertight doors to be closed then turned to Fourth Officer Boxhall to order him to take soundings. Even as the young officer turned to go, however, the ship's carpenter arrived on the bridge to report 'She's making water fast'.

Funnel for auxiliary Machinery & ventilation

SPACE OCCUPIED BY RECIPROCATING & TURBINE ENGINES

WATER LINE

3. Forward Funnels carrying off Product of Combustion from Main Boilers

SPACE OCCUPIED BY BOILERS

Far Left: views of the luxurious interior of the *Titanic*. Left: Artist's impression of the boat tilting into the Atlantic

Those of the passengers still awake were unaware that anything had occurred, for the impact had been slight. Lawrence Beesley, one of the survivors, stated that there was 'no sound of a crash or of anything else; no sense of shock, no jar that felt like one heavy body meeting another . . .'

Up on deck, despite the bitter cold, some energetic passengers were actually having a 'snowball' fight, using the ice that the deadly berg had deposited during the brief encounter, while one, obviously a wag and not wishing to leave the comfort of the lounge, held out his glass and asked a friend to 'see if any ice has come aboard; I would like some for this.'

A few passengers asked stewards why the engines had stopped, and were assured that there was nothing wrong. The stewards were acting in good faith – at that moment they truly believed that nothing *was* wrong. Down below, however, it was a different story. The men in the foremost boiler-room found themselves swimming as tons of water began to thrust through a great rent in the ship's side. They managed to struggle into the next boiler-room, and then the next, to reach No. 4 which was nearly amidships but still dry.

Realizing that the damage was severe, Captain Smith went to the radio-room where the two Marconi men Jack Phillips and Harold Bride were now on stand-by, to tell them that the ship had struck an iceberg and he wished them to be ready to send out a distress call.

By the time he had regained the bridge it was obvious that the *Titanic* was slowly sinking. The berg had ripped a jagged gash along the liner's starboard bow for one-third of her length, and the ice-cold Atlantic water was pouring in. At 0025, some 25 minutes after the collision, Captain Smith ordered the boats to be uncovered. Ten minutes later he returned to the radio-room to order the operators to start transmitting, adding grimly: 'It may be your last chance.' Immediately the urgent call was crackling into the night, stating what had happened, giving the ship's call-sign MGY and her position, and asking for immediate help.

It was picked up by two liners, the *Frankfort* and the *Carpathia*, although the captain of the latter twice asked his operator if he had read the message

---

Sabotage on luxury liner

On her maiden voyage, the sumptuous French liner, the *Georges Philippar* was completely destroyed by fires which apparently broke out simultaneously in several parts of the vessel. Sabotage was blamed for the mysterious disaster, which occurred in the Red Sea in May 1930 and claimed 53 lives.

The *Titanic* being towed out of Southampton Port on its departure for New York. Inset: Millionaire, John Jacob Astor, one of the 1,403 people who perished

correctly, not believing that the unsinkable *Titanic* could be in such trouble. When reassured that it was, he ordered his operator to reply that he would be coming to the rescue at full speed, and asked his engineers to give him 'everything that they had'.

Meanwhile the *Titanic*'s stewards were going from cabin to cabin, tapping on the doors and almost apologetically asking the occupants to put on warm clothing and go to their boat stations, taking their life-belts with them. Still unaware of the seriousness of the situation, most of the passengers did as they were asked although some refused to leave the warmth of their cabins merely for an unexpected and very inconsiderate drill.

The boats were swung out and the order was passed: 'Women and children only'. At first there was great reluctance to leave the ship for she seemed so safe, so permanent, compared to the frail-looking boats. As Beesley was to state later: 'The sea was as calm as an inland lake save for the

---

Tragedy of the 'boat people'

Nearly 700 Vietnamese refugees died in a series of disasters off the Malaysian coast during 1978 and 1979. An overloaded ship sank on 26 July 1978, killing 217 people. On 22 November 1979, a trawler hit a sandbar in the Tregganu estuary after being refused permission to land, and 200 of the 254 aboard drowned. Another 250 'boat people' died in three further disasters in the following month.

---

gentle swell which could impart no motion to a ship the size of the *Titanic*. To stand on the deck many feet above the water lapping idly against her sides, gave one a sense of wonderful security . . .'

Everyone was behaving in a calm, almost detached manner. There was none of the panic which was to cause loss of life in other ships under similar circumstances, although a brief and ugly scene among the steerage passengers was quickly quelled by the officers.

At last the boats began to be loaded and then slowly lowered, but not actually dropped into the sea. This was because Captain Smith had been told of the replies to his distress signal, especially that from the *Carpathia* which had stated that she was only 60 miles away and would be with them within four hours. But the captain soon realized that his ship was sinking lower with every passing minute, and as her bows went deeper and her stern rose from the water it would be more difficult to lower the boats. Some were still only half-filled, many women refusing to leave their husbands. Mrs Isador Strauss was one, saying firmly, 'Where you go, I go.' They stayed together – and died together.

As the boats splashed down, the strains of 'Nearer my God to Thee' drifted into the night from a group of the ship's musicians who had gathered on deck with their instruments. Some of the male passengers joined in the singing, others stared over the ship's side for a last lingering look at the faces of their loved ones before they became indistinguishable in the darkness. The crews of the boats were mainly stewards and stokers, for every officer and nearly every seaman stayed on board to help those who remained.

Two hours after the liner had been struck Captain Smith ordered 'Abandon ship! Every man for himself!' He remained on his bridge and was never seen again. Despite this order, Phillips and Bride were still transmitting, urging the ships that were straining to their rescue to hurry. Then their power failed and they went on deck.

Those in the lifeboats looked back at the sinking liner. The ship, nearly a sixth of a mile long with four towering funnels and still brilliant with light that gleamed from portholes and saloons, was now down by the bows and sinking slowly but discernibly. The angle became wider as her stern lifted, then she tilted to attain an almost vertically upright position and remained thus, motionless. As she swung all her lights were suddenly extinguished and there came a deep rumble as tons of machinery broke loose and fell towards the bows. Then the great liner slid forwards and down, the waters closing over her like a shroud.

Soon after 0400 hours the *Carpathia*, having raced through dangerous waters at (for her) a hitherto unknown speed of 17 knots, arrived on the scene and by 0800 hours had rescued every boatload. With her was the *California*, a liner that had stopped during the night less than 10 miles from the *Titanic* and whose captain was subsequently severely criticized for not observing the stricken vessel's distress rockets.

The whole world was stunned when the final accounting was released. Of the 2,206 people on board, 1,403 were lost, mostly crew and male passengers. Yet out of the greatest sea disaster of all time came good. The inquiry resulted in the formation of the International Ice Patrol and also stricter Board of Trade regulations regarding the provision of sufficient lifeboats to carry everyone on board ships.

Tokyo Earthquake (1923)

On Sunday, 2 September 1923, a news report came via Shanghai from Osaka, Japan. It read: 'Yesterday, Yokohama and most of Tokyo totally destroyed in devastating earthquake followed by fire. Heavy loss of life.'

For some days, because of shattered communications, news of what had happened reached the outside world only in fragments.

On 3 September, more reports trickled through: '100,000 people reported killed, 200,000 buildings destroyed, including all Tokyo's business quarter and most government offices. A power station collapsed, killing 600. Tokyo arsenal exploded. Water system completely destroyed. Food warehouses burned to the ground. Fires still raging.'

On 4 September: 'Casualties mounting, possibly 150,000 killed. Railway station in ruins; Japan's longest tunnel at Sasako caved in, suffocating a trainload of passengers. Sumida River burst its banks, drowning hundreds. All bridges down. Almost all schools, hospitals, factories wrecked. Summer resorts on Sagami Bay (20 miles south-west of Tokyo) obliterated.'

On 5 September: 'Many passenger and goods trains derailed with heavy loss of life. Tidal waves, 40 feet high, swamped Sagami Bay, causing massive destruction, then receded, baring the ocean floor. Oil-storage tanks at Yokohama exploded. 40,000 people burned to death by fire cyclone in Tokyo park. 1,600 crushed, then burned in subsequent fire when Fuji cotton mill collapsed. American hospital thrown bodily with all its inmates from cliffs above Yokohama. Count Yamamoto, recently appointed Prime Minister, was attempting to form a cabinet at Tokyo Naval Club when the floor gave way, killing 20 of his colleagues. Estimated casualties: 500,000 homeless of whom many injured. Total dead, in population of 3,000,000, unknown. 1,500 prisoners released from the Ichigaya prison, Tokyo, when the building was threatened with collapse and more have broken out from other prisons. There is now widespread robbery with violence, looting of abandoned premises, rape and motiveless murder. This has been blamed, apparently unjustly, on several thousand Korean immigrants living in the city and some hundreds have been lynched. Martial law has been declared.'

By 6 September, the London *Times* correspondent reported that Yokohama had been 'wiped off the map'. In Tokyo there were now one and a half million homeless. 'The difficulty of telling such a vast story is to know where to begin.'

The horror had begun at 10 minutes before noon on the hot, sunlit morning of Saturday when the first earthquake shock, more powerful than any felt in 70 years, struck Tokyo and the port of Yokohama, eight miles to the south-west of the outer fringe of the city on the shore of Tokyo Bay.

The islands of Japan, lying within the south-east Asian seismic belt and perched on the edge of the great Pacific trench known as the Tuscarora Deep, suffered thousands of shocks every year and building methods had been adapted accordingly. In Tokyo in 1923 there were some western-style ferro-concrete buildings linked by broad roads near the centre, but the rest of the city was still one gigantic village with narrow twisting paths running between small, one-storey homes clustered closely together and made in a traditional style of lightweight timber, paper and thatch. The beams in these houses were not nailed but dove-tailed together so that when earth-tremors became heavy the inhabitants could simply dismantle the structure.

But in 1923 disaster was beyond control. In Tokyo, the first shock, followed by two others equally massive, destroyed even newer buildings and left the terrain like a corrugated roof with the raised parts eight or nine feet above the normal level. Huge chasms opened in the streets swallowing up people, even tram-cars, then closing on them like a giant mouth. Telephone wires and overhead electric cables were snapped like string, people tripping over them in their panic being electrocuted; an entire tram-load died in this way, struck rigid, according to an eye-witness, as they had been in their last moment of life. 'We saw them sitting in their seats, all in natural attitudes. One woman's hand was held out with a coin as though she had been on the point of paying her fare.'

China rocked by earthquakes

An estimated 1,400,000 people died in 1976 when earthquakes shattered one of China's most densely-populated regions. The first shock, at 3.42 a.m. on 28 July, was measured at 8.2 on the Richter scale, equal to 10,000 Hiroshima atom bombs. The shock waves were felt 3,500 miles away in Alaska. A second major quake 15 hours later was followed by 125 tremors over the next three months. The industrial city of Tangshan was totally destroyed, with 655,000 dead and 780,000 injured. Two-thirds of the buildings in Tientsin were either demolished or too dangerous to re-occupy. In Peking, many buildings were damaged, and up to 100 people died. Four hundred years earlier, China's Shensi province suffered the world's record losses from a single 'quake. A total of 830,000 people perished in a two-hour shock on 23 January 1556.

TOKYO EARTHQUAKE

Above: huge crators appeared as a
result of the earthquake
Left: The flimsy structure of the
buildings meant that homes were
completely flattened

The earthquake was not the deadliest killer. Fire, caused largely by exploding gas-mains, destroyed thousands more. Driven by a strong wind the flames were soon roaring through the city. Hordes of terrified people tried to escape into the large grounds surrounding the Imperial Palace, even into canals where they stood for hours, only to be found later dead, their heads charred beyond recognition and the rest of their bodies intact. One woman was lucky: she stood neck-high in water with a baby on her head for a whole day, and both survived. Elsewhere some young girls were found cowering inside a large drain-pipe. Others had thought themselves safe in Tokyo's many parks but freak conditions produced whirling funnels of flame which swept across great distances to snatch hundreds of victims high in the air and fling them incinerated to earth again.

For the first 36 hours, people could do no more than try to survive. Large numbers of troops for clearance work, military engineers and relief supplies were on the way, but help from beyond Japan took time to organize. Meanwhile the fires could not be stopped, even by blowing up buildings in their path, and on the Saturday night, beneath a sky that itself seemed on fire in a dome of scarlet and orange above the stricken city, pathetic groups huddled wherever they could find space to breathe, clutching the few belongings they had managed to salvage. Some wandered about near where their homes had been with the names of missing children, relatives and friends scrawled on bits of paper which they held out to strangers or hung from their necks, because their throats were too parched to be able to speak. On the following night, Sunday, when the fires were dying for lack of fuel, people were seen still searching, groping about with little paper lanterns on poles, their mouths covered against clouds of choking white dust that the wind was whipping across smouldering ruins.

In Yokohama the scene was equally horrifying. Yet the purely physical destruction was not as tragic as in Tokyo which, under its former name of Edo, had been inhabited for 4,000 years and contained many cultural treasures. Seventeen libraries were destroyed in the fire, including that of the Imperial Palace, as well as 151 Shinto shrines, 633 Buddhist temples and

Horror in Chile

Four thousand people died when earthquakes hit southern Chile on 21 May 1960, and partly demolished the town of Concepción for the fifth time in its history. Tidal waves caused by the seismic upheaval also drowned 180 people and caused millions of pounds worth of damage in Japan, 10,000 miles away.

TOKYO EARTHQUAKE

many beautiful gardens brought to perfection by that particular Japanese talent for creating a botanical paradise.

Yokohama, a modern, struggling port with hardly anything old or picturesque about it, but economically most important, was also struck by the earthquake and fire which occurred almost simultaneously. The first great shock which sent the American hospital and many luxurious homes toppling from The Bluff also buckled the quays into snake-like convolutions, wrecked a long pier stretching out into the Bay, destroyed the customs house at its head, tore chasms in the streets, shattered bridges, demolished the two big hotels burying 180 guests, and ripped open the oil tanks.

As the second and third shocks quickly followed, crowds of terrified people stampeded to the shore expecting to find safety in small boats, only to see a wall of blazing oil spreading inexorably towards them across the water. Many were burned, others rowed frantically towards the *Empress of Australia*, at that moment being drawn by tugs out of the Bay, and ultimately 12,000 were picked up by the liner. 21,000 died in Yokohama that day.

Final estimates of the total dead in both cities were around 150,000, and of the severely injured, 100,000. Apart from larger buildings, some of which

Soldiers serving rations
to starving survivors

Earthquake in Rumania

More than 1,500 people died when an earthquake hit the Transylvania region of Rumania, north of Bucharest, on 4 March 1977. But one 19-year-old boy was rescued alive in Bucharest after being entombed by rubble for ten days.

had stood up well, 700,000 small homes had been destroyed. No one even tried to assess the financial and economic loss. The rescue services, principally the army, and the survivors themselves fought back strongly. At first, there was only a handful of rice for each person each day, and one correspondent noted that a man he knew to have been 'worth millions' was grateful to get even that. But supplies from outlying districts built up quickly and until the telephone system was restored the army ran a carrier-pigeon service with other cities to make known the local needs. Thousands of the homeless were evacuated; tents were provided for the remainder. Within days some water mains had been repaired and in the following weeks, helped by a government scheme for compensation, many small businessmen were back, setting up shop again.

Massive aid came from many countries, including Britain and U.S.A., in money, emergency supplies and medical teams, and within seven years Tokyo and Yokohama had been completely rebuilt. By 1930 they were new cities with barely a scar.

Today, having risen once more phoenix-like from their ashes, the capital city and its port are only part of a continuous urban-industrial belt containing the largest concentration of population in Japan. Experts say that even reasonable safety from earthquakes has not yet been achieved – and perhaps it never will be.

The R101 (1930) and the Hindenburg (1937)

The airship industry is probably the only industry to die in modern times because of disasters, although it experienced only two, the *R101* and the *Hindenberg*, which had a combined death-toll of less than 100. There have been much worse disasters, on land, at sea and in the air, but none has brought to such an abrupt halt the industry from which it evolved. Perhaps the seeds of disaster lay not in its flying machines, but in the industry itself, with its vulnerable technology resting upon politics.

It was not a young industry: the rigid airship evolved from the non-rigid blimp, and that in turn came from the ordinary balloon. Manned balloons were used by the French more than 200 years ago, and in wartime had obvious reconnaissance functions, but as they were largely at the mercy of the wind it became obvious that an elongated envelope propelled by an engine was essential if such dirigibles were to prove tactically useful.

The first truly successful airship, designed by Frenchman H. Giffard, was steam-powered and could offer a speed of 5 mph in still air. A more practical electrically-powered machine named *La France* took to the air in 1884. From then on designs improved until, in the period 1910 to World War I, the German Zeppelin pioneered air travel by safely carrying some tens of thousands of passengers over a distance of several million miles.

Although progress was made mainly by Germany and France, Britain had produced a few non-rigid airships (the first rigid machine, *The Mayflower*, crashed on its maiden flight). World War I demonstrated the success of the Zeppelin in air raids, but also its weaknesses (in particular the use of hydrogen as a lifting gas as the U.S.A. would not export non-inflammable helium), but it was from a forced-down Zeppelin in 1916 that Britain, copying the basic design, started serious work on its own rigid airships. Meanwhile the much smaller blimp had become fashionable as an observation post, especially for submarine detection. By the end of the war the airship industry had a rather healthy look about it.

By 1919 Britain had built two rigid airships – the *R33* and the *R34*. Defeated Germany was prevented from making any more Zeppelins until 1926, but had nevertheless been studying some of the more sophisticated problems involved.

Then came the two disasters – seven years apart – that virtually put a stop to airship manufacture in every country in the world. In 1930 came the destruction of Britain's *R101* (47 dead) followed, in 1937, by the more dramatically publicized *Hindenberg* disaster (36 dead). Germany kept its *Graf Zeppelin* in passenger service for another year, but World War II was imminent and it was already obvious that the battlefield of the air would in future be dominated by the much faster and more manoeuverable heavier-than-air machines, and that bombers, as they were made bigger and adapted for troop transport, would form the nucleus of civil aviation to come.

Although the use of airships as a slow-speed form of transportation for

The Wreckage of the R101

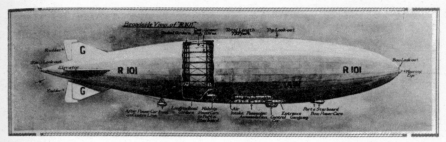

Diagram of the R101

heavy freight today has its protagonists, most people regard the 'gasbag' era as dead. The process of dying began with the *R101* and the subsequent breaking-up for scrap of the better-designed *R100*.

In 1924 the British Government decided to stop toying with airships and moved seriously into the industry with the construction of the *R100* and the *R101*. The *R100* would be built by the Airship Guarantee Company, a subsidiary of Vickers at Howden in Yorkshire, while the *R101* was to be manufactured by the Air Ministry itself, at Cardington in Bedfordshire. The *R100*'s builders were short of cash but long on expertise, being able to call on Dr Barnes Wallis of subsequent 'Dam-buster' fame, and many other top-ranking scientists and engineers including Nevile Shute (*No Highway*) Norway, whose first two names became a household word.

The Ministry, however, suffered from lack of designing talent, as many of its experienced men had been killed in the war. It also suffered from over-exposure in the press as, with taxpayers' money involved, every stage in the work at Cardington had to be publicized. Thus, errors which the Airship Guarantee Company was able to rectify in silence had to be retained – for example, the too-heavy British diesel engines which the A.G.C. quietly swopped for lighter, petrol-driven power units.

Troubles and arguments, both technical and political, ended with the *R101* slower by 10 mph at 71 mph and, at 25 tons, with only half the disposable lift of her sister ship. The airship was flown to the Hendon Air Display in the summer of 1930 to let the public admire her, but only experts could have known she was losing gas and that she would only be able to return to Cardington by throwing out huge amounts of ballast. It was there that drastic and, in the event, foolish action was prescribed: instead of taking steps to reduce weight it was decided to increase it by cutting the airship in half, inserting a new metal bay (thus adding to her length) and putting in more bags of hydrogen for lift.

A photograph of the R101, swinging from the mooring-mast at Cardington

While all this was going on, the privately built *R100* made a very successful flight to Canada. Air Minister Lord Thompson, perhaps somewhat put out, decreed brusquely that *R101* would leave for India via Egypt on 4 October, with himself on board. By then the airship would be 'safe as a house, save for the millionth chance' – and anyway, he had to get back on time for a meeting. This was all very impressive, though it is not known to what extent Thomson's enthusiasm was generally shared.

The largely untested *R101* left its Cardington mast on the ordained date with 54 people aboard, of whom only six were passengers. In these days of plastic synthetics it is difficult to realize that the dural frame contained 17 hydrogen-filled gasbags made from the membrane of bullocks' intestines, held in position by hundreds of wires. New valves were fitted to control the gas, but they tended to 'over-react' causing them to release gas at an unexpected air turbulence, thus releasing gas prematurely. This was one of many control problems.

Despite efforts to save overall weight, no limit was placed on personal luggage; Lord Thompson's private effects weighed as much as 24 people. The airship's fittings included silver cutlery, potted palms and 600 feet of heavy Axminster carpeting. Supplies of food and drink were lavish, as there was to be an aerial state banquet over Ismailia, with Egyptian notables and other distinguished figures as guests. Because of the inconvenience of refuelling during a banquet (no smoking, etc.) the ship was carrying nine more tons of diesel oil than she needed to reach her destination.

Small wonder that the *R101* shuddered painfully into the sky that evening. A resident of Hitchin later told the *Daily Express* that she had run out of her house to find everything lit by 'a ghastly red and green light . . . there was the *R101* heading straight for the house . . . she cleared the trees of our drive and the house by the smallest margin . . . as the green and red tail-lights moved away up the drive horror descended on us all.'

THE R101 AND THE HINDENBERG

A few hours later Le Bourget airport in France confirmed that the airship was one kilometre north of Beauvais. After 2.07 a.m. the *R101* stopped replying to wireless messages, and by 2.08 horrified villagers had been woken by the noise and then the inferno. Le Bourget's operator tapped out the words, '*G-FAAW a pris feu*'.

G-FAAW – *R101* – had indeed caught fire, as a result of not clearing a low hill at Beauvais. It was all over in minutes. Unlike the more fortunate *Hindenburg*, there was no chance for passengers and most of the crew, for they were sleeping. Seven crew members survived.

No one knows for certain why the *R101* hit the ground at Beauvais. Perhaps she broke up under aerodynamic stress, perhaps a gas bag punctured, perhaps she simply lacked sufficient lift. Whatever the cause, it ended Britain's contribution to the development of the airship. *R100* was immediately grounded, then broken up for scrap.

That was almost the death of the airship industry as a whole, but not quite. The Germans continued, and by 1936 had completed the *Hindenberg* to join its sister ship *Graf Zeppelin*. With a length of rather more than 800 feet, she was the biggest airship ever built. Power came from four mighty Daimler diesel engines driving propellers in separate gondolas under the great gas-lifted hull. As with all airships, the gas was contained in a quantity of separate bags, or cells. Today, those would be made completely gas-tight, but in 1937 a slow seepage was expected and allowed for.

This brought with it the danger of fire, but designers had perfected the interior passenger quarters, with their 25 two-berth cabins, spacious dining-room, saloon and reading-room, so that there was almost no risk of hydrogen entering. Smoking was confined to one absolutely safe room, with double-doors and an ingenious method of keeping its air pressure higher than elsewhere, so that no gas could possibly enter. Passengers could smoke freely here, though the cigarette-lighters were chained to tables to prevent the absent-minded taking them to their bedrooms.

Plane explodes

An airliner exploded 9,000 feet over the Peruvian jungle on 24 December 1971, causing the deaths of 91 passengers and crew. There was only one survivor. Seventeen-year-old Juliane Keopcke was trapped in a section of the plane which, as it fell to earth, was caught in the strong updraught of a tropical storm. Her landing being cushioned, she escaped death and survived ten days before being discovered by natives.

Air crash above San Diego

One hundred and fifty people died when a Pacific South-West Airlines Boeing 727 approaching Lindbergh Field collided with a light Cessna 172 plane 3,000 feet above San Diego, California, on 25 September 1978. Fifteen homes were set ablaze by falling wreckage.

Elsewhere, in this ingenious, luxurious ship, was a baby grand piano, made of aluminium. On either side were promenade decks from which passengers could look out and down through big sloping windows.

The *Hindenberg* made a number of flights to the United States and to Brazil during 1936–37, and May 1937 brought yet another scheduled departure from Frankfurt to the American terminus at Lakehurst. Nothing could have been more routine; no German passenger airship or Zeppelin had yet crashed. From those first flights in 1910, many thousands of people had been carried safely to their destinations.

Slowly she rose into Frankfurt's sky on the evening of 3 May. Her passenger accommodation was half empty (though it was almost fully booked for the return trip) and the 36 on board, with a standard crew, totalled 97. Estimated time of arrival at Lakehurst was 8 a.m. on the 6th, but very soon Captain Max Pruss realized that strong headwinds were going to upset the schedule.

It was already 15.30 on the 6th when *Hindenberg* passed over New York's Empire State Building – a regular practice, to advertise Germany and her great airship to the people below, and give passengers an exciting, unfamiliar, look at the city. However, what interest there might have been in the arrival of another airship flight was diminished, rather than heightened, by its lateness. Apart from passengers' friends and relatives, few people were heading for Lakehurst. Hardly any of the press were turning out; one radio company had sent a commentator, Herb Morrison, with a portable recorder.

Bad weather made Pruss delay his arrival still further, and it was not until 7.00 p.m. that he began his approach to the Lakehurst mooring-mast.

The first lines were dropped to the ground crew at 7.25 p.m. A slightly bored Herb Morrison began his commentary, unaware that it would become one of the most moving records of human anguish.

There was a flame, and Morrison's voice, abruptly kindling with it to hysteria, sobbed, 'It's broken into flames, it's flashing, flashing, flashing terribly, it's bursting into flames!'

Those inside were the last to know, and to this day no one can be sure what

The *Hindenburg* burning fiercely on the landing field at Lakehurst

THE R101 AND THE HINDENBERG

The *Hindenberg* passing over New York City

caused that flame. Miraculously, with seven million cubic feet of incandescent hydrogen about them, only 36 died out of *Hindenburg*'s airborne total of 97. Much credit for this must go to officers and men at Lakehurst, who risked death to lead shocked, hurt, passengers and crew out of the holocaust.

So ended the day of the passenger airship. The rest of the world, including Britain, which had been watching the Germans with interest, gave up hope that these monsters of the sky would ever be safe and practical. There were undoubtedly other unspoken considerations, for no industry could die with such a small casualty list. The Germans withdrew the perfectly safe *Graf Zeppelin* in 1938, and in retrospect the reason is obvious. Zeppelins were not war machines. Balloons and blimps continued, however, while the real hardware of fighters and bombers took over.

There remains the possible return of the airship for freight transportation. Independent of land or sea it can travel 'as the crow flies', which offers advantages. In the long term, the issue will be decided by sheer economics, for a freight airship must make a profit if it is to survive – or even become a reality.

The Morro Castle (1934)

The *Morro Castle* was a vessel of 11,520 tons, pride of the Ward Line of America, dignified and stately, beautifully furnished and equipped, and only four years old. Although originally designed as a 'ferry' running between New York and Havana, she had become a popular cruising liner for those seeking sun, sea and relaxation and also an escape from the rigours of prohibition of the time. For no illicit speak-easy 'bath-tub' liquor was drunk on board *her*. Everything – spirits, wines and liqueurs – was imported and was the real thing. Consequently the trip to Havana and back was, as many regulars agreed, 'one helluva cruise.'

The final night of each voyage was inevitably the wildest and noisiest of them all with everyone making the most of the last night of riotous freedom before arriving in New York at eight o'clock on the following morning.

Even the repeal of prohibition in the previous year made no difference – the last night in the *Morro Castle* was, by tradition, an abandoned, uninhibited affair and this particular night of Friday 7 September 1934 was no exception. Many of the passengers had been having last-minute parties in their cabins and were arriving in the warm, perfumed and rich-food-scented atmosphere of the main dining-room. Only at the captain's table where a number of the privileged had assembled was there a slight note of discord. The guests were there, but where was their host, Captain Robert Willmott? While they waited, undecided whether to start without him, a page-boy arrived with the captain's apologies – he could not attend for the moment. Actually the popular, English-born captain was already dead from a heart attack and had been found a little earlier by his second-in-command, Chief Officer William Warms, lying slumped, half-dressed, over his bath.

The inevitable rumours began to spread around the room until an officer announced what had happened and that Warms had taken over command of the ship. The sad news effectively ended the evening's festivities. The orchestra left the stand, lights were dimmed and the public rooms slowly emptied, although parties still continued in the cabins. It was said later that several girls had to be carried back, insensible, to their own cabins and that some members of the crew were fired for being drunk.

Up on the bridge, Warms stared into the night, conscious of the responsibility of this, his first command. A strong north-easter was building up, rain was lashing across the decks and vivid lightning was illuminating the dark, churning waves. At 2.00 a.m. the ship altered course for the Ambrose Light and New York harbour and Warms relaxed; another six hours would see the ship at Pier 13 and the present ordeal over.

Then with terrifying suddenness, a report reached the bridge from a night watchman who had seen smoke drifting from a ventilator. An officer sent to investigate returned white-faced and shaken. A fierce fire was already raging in the ship's library and a steward, opening a locker, had staggered back as a great gout of flame leaped from its interior. He had then run to one of the levers which controlled the ship's elaborate fire-control system and pulled hard. Nothing happened.

From that moment the liner was doomed.

Even as the alarm was being raised, a great mushroom of smoke and flame was rising high above the ship's superstructure, sparks and cinders raining down upon her decks. For the most part the ship's crew was unable to cope with the situation. A good number were stewards – ship-borne waiters – many of whom used the liner as an easy way of life, some even for a little lucrative smuggling on the side, and their first thought was for themselves. It turned out later that in the first six lifeboats, with a total capacity of more than 400, which pulled into Spring Lake, New Jersey, there were only 85 survivors, of whom 80 were members of the crew. Among them was the ship's chief engineer, Eben Abbott, whose immediate responsibility should have been to see that the hoses had ample power to operate. Instead, he was away in the very first boat.

For those experienced officers and seamen who remained, the subsequent hours became an unbelievable nightmare. Panic had spread amongst the passengers who refused, for the most part, to obey orders and make for the boats. A crew member said later, 'They wouldn't leave. We pleaded with them. We tried to herd them together. Many tried to fight their way past us and get down the ladder to the lower deck. At last we were forced to leave without them, as sparks and cinders were burning the ropes . . . I told the passengers plainly that they must run the risk of getting singed in going to the boats. They did not seem to understand. We got the boats away in the nick of time, or we should all have been burned.'

But as they rowed away in the near-empty lifeboats they left the confused and panic-stricken passengers to fend for themselves. The scenes were indescribable in their horror. Men, women and children milled about the deck in a bizarre variety of clothing. Some were in pyjamas and nightgowns, others, who a little while before had been enjoying some private party, were in evening attire, the women in elegant gowns and with jewels that sparkled in the glow of the fire. They began to huddle together as the flames drew closer and then, as the pitch between the deck planking began to bubble with

THE MORRO CASTLE

The Doomed *Morro Castle*, beached and on fire at Asbury Port, New Jersey

the heat, began to perform a grotesque *danse macabre* before finally plunging over the side with cries of utter despair.

Soon the flame-lit, heaving water around the liner seemed filled with passengers, mixed in utter confusion, clinging to wreckage or to the few rafts that had been launched. On one occasion a lifeboat, manned by only eight of the crew, passed through a group of men and women who shouted for help and clutched desperately at the gunwales, but the boat moved relentlessly on to disappear into the darkness. Of the 318 passengers, 90 were to die; of the 231 crew, 44.

George Rogers, the chief radio operator, was seated at his instrument, desperately awaiting the return of his first assistant, George Alagna, whom he had sent to the bridge for permission to start transmitting an SOS. As he sat, a wet towel over his face, he watched as paint began to peel off the walls and as a curtain caught fire and dropped down, setting fire to a settee. Soon he could hardly breathe. Finally, after Alagna had returned with a negative and had been sent back again, he tapped out the CQ (Stand by) then continued his agonizing wait. At last Alagna staggered back into the radio cabin and said, 'Okay chief, start sending.'

This was half-an-hour after the fire had first been reported. Precious time had been lost.

Rogers began to tap out his distress call: SOS. SOS. KGOV. TWENTY

MILES SOUTH OF SCOTLAND LIGHT. Halfway through a repeat of this message, an explosion rocked the cabin as the batteries blew out, filling the room with fumes of sulphuric acid. Coughing and spluttering, he managed to turn on his auxiliary generator and then tapped out: SOS TWENTY MILES SOUTH OF SCOTLAND LIGHT. CANNOT WORK MUCH LONGER. FIRE DIRECTLY UNDER RADIO. NEED ASSISTANCE IMMEDIATELY.

Another explosion effectively ended all further transmission but the message had been received by several ships in the vicinity and dawn revealed the great bulk of the *Monarch of Bermuda*, together with the *City of Savannah*, *Andrea F. Luckenbach* and others, all answering the call. The *Monarch of Bermuda* was the nearest vessel and her captain, Albert Francis 'saw a lot of men on the poop deck of the *Morro Castle* hanging over the side and yelling for assistance.' He and others on his ship also saw an incredible sight. Many of the *Morro Castle*'s passengers, trapped in their cabins, had tried to escape by squeezing through the portholes. These were far too small, however, and most of the desperate people had become helplessly stuck, the expressions on their faces revealing the agony of being burnt alive. As a passenger on the *Monarch of Bermuda* said: 'The grimaces made by the people in agony at the portholes was something that I shall never forget. On the deck we saw a young fellow with his wife. She fainted in his arms, and a huge tongue of flame popped out from the wall and sucked them in. We saw a man in pyjamas go up like a torch . . .'

By noon the only signs of life aboard the fiercely burning liner was in her bows where Warms and a few of his men were now stationed. A coastguard cutter, the *Tampa*, nosed as near as it dared and offered to take them off, but Warms refused – his ship was still afloat, he said. This offer was repeated several times but each time Warms replied, 'Not until the *Morro Castle* is in tow.'

The ship was held by an anchor which had been dropped to stop her colliding with rescue ships and this had to be weighed before the ship could be towed away, but there was no power, no winches. Two of Warm's men, however, had small hacksaws in their pockets, and for the next five hours they laboriously sawed through the three-inch anchor-cable, finally freeing the vessel. A hawser was then passed across but snapped as the storm increased.

One by one, the 14 crewmen, including a 14-year-old bell-boy who had elected to stay with them, were finally taken off. At last Warms also agreed to leave his ship and board the *Tampa*, but only after the commander had threatened to use force. Another hawser was passed and the tow began. At first all went well, the cutter towing ahead and a pilot boat acting as a jury rudder astern, but when both ropes parted the liner was abandoned to slowly drift shorewards, still burning furiously, with her paint peeling off in swathes from her once glossy sides, listing at an angle of 30 degrees. Narrowly missing a pier, she came to rest near the broadwalk at Asbury Park, between New York and Atlantic City, a popular convention and 'fun' town on the Atlantic seaboard.

News of the disaster had already been heard on the radio and by first light a dense crowd of sightseers had assembled to stare seawards as the flame and smoke-blackened liner drifted towards the shore. By noon, owners of ice-cream stalls, hot-dog and frozen-custard stands were eagerly coaxing every cent from this out-of-season show; families stood watching, while bodies were carried up the beach as they were washed ashore. Hawkers also moved amongst the steadily increasing crowds selling pieces of 'genuine' wreckage at a dollar a time.

By early afternoon the crowd had increased to a quarter of a million people and squads of regular soldiers, armed with rifles, were rushed to the scene to drive the mob like sheep before them and establish safety zones around the place where the ship lay beached. Scores of reporters also arrived and the stories they gathered were extremely harrowing.

An inquiry was soon opened before a Federal Grand Jury and proved to be a particularly outspoken one. Warms faced a number of charges, including failure to exercize discipline and control; to arouse the passengers or provide them with lifebelts; to organize the crew to escort the passengers to the boats; to fight the fire; and failure to send out the SOS promptly. He also came in for special criticism when it was disclosed that the liner had been allowed to steam at full speed into a steady head wind which helped fan the flames. Warms, Chief Engineer Abbott and Henry E. Cabaud, executive vice-president of the Ward Line, were arrested, found guilty and sentenced to imprisonment. This sentence, however, was set aside on appeal. The Line itself was fined $10,000 and also had to settle claims amounting to nearly a million dollars.

The inquiry did not establish the cause of the fire. Most experts agreed that a carelessly dropped cigarette had been responsible; others believed that the funnel passing close behind the library walls had overheated them. The loss of life was more simply explained. It was due to naked, uncontrollable panic. On the part of the passengers this was understandable: thrust suddenly into a situation where a horrible death threatened from red fire or black water, their loss of control was excusable.

For Warms, an experienced seaman, there was no such excuse. Faced with sudden responsibility involving his first command and the lives of his passengers and crew, he also cracked, but in a less obvious way. Alagna said

Acting Commander, R. W. Hodge brings the body of a young boy to shore

at the trial that Warms was 'behaving like a madman'. When the crisis came, he was unable to cope.

That was not the end of the story. The 'hero', Rogers, for a time earned his living recounting the events of that fateful night in vaudeville theatres throughout the U.S.A., but was later convicted of attempted murder and died in gaol. His assistant, Alagna, whose evidence against Warms helped convict that unfortunate officer, later tried to commit suicide.

Not long afterwards the once majestic vessel was towed to Baltimore to be scrapped. She had originally cost five million dollars; she was sold for less than $34,000. Her name passed into history as the principal in one of the ghastliest sea tragedies of all time.

Naples Black Market Express (1944)

World War II provided the most bizarre railway catastrophe of all time. Train No. 8017, which ran between Naples and Lucania every Thursday night, was known as the Black Market Express. It carried 520 passengers, most of them the professional black marketeers of Naples who made this regular journey to fill their bags with meats, grains, vegetables, oils, tobacco and sweets for Naples, then (in March 1944) occupied by the Allied Forces.

Although *la borsa nera* (the black market) was prohibited, the Allied Military Government and the Italian officials realized that if these black marketeers did not use Train 8017 to bring in illegal supplies, there would be hardly enough food available for the million inhabitants of Naples.

On the night of 2 March 1944, the train pulled out of Naples with 521 passengers and six railway workers: the 8017 had 42 box-cars (empty), two steam-engines, four coaches and one caboose. On all its previous trips two engines had been used, as the total weight of the train had never exceeded 500 tons but, on this fateful journey, medical students from Bari were returning from a hospital field exercise. Total weight touched 511 tons – 11 tons over the maximum for a two-engine pull.

The 8017 might have got away with the overloading, but some parts of the Naples-Lucania line had stretches of ice-coated upgrade rails. If it had not attempted to hit top speed on these stretches the chances were that the slippery tracks would have proved impassable.

After it pulled out of Balvano-Ricigliano station on the Apennine Mountain chain, the station-master said goodnight to his staff and left some instructions with his assistant, Giuseppe Salonia, for his spell of duty. These done, Salonia curled up with his newspaper for the next hour or so. Just before the next train was scheduled to enter Balvano, he remembered that he had not received any ticker-tape message about the 8017's arrival at Bella-Muro, its next stop nearly four miles further on, thus telling Salonia that the single track would be all clear for use.

Instead, Salonia was told by the Bella-Muro station that the 8017 was running nearly two hours late. He replied that he would hold the 8025 at Balvano and would check the single track himself with a free locomotive. At 2.40 a.m. the 8025 rumbled into the station. Salonia ordered two trackmen,

Caponegro and Biondi, to detach the engine from the train so that he could inspect the track leading to Bella-Muro.

The big mystery was the fate of the 8017 from the time it left Balvano station. Moments before it drew out, the train's chief engineer, Gigliani, in the leading engine had ordered his fireman, Rosario Barbato, to shovel a particularly large dosage of coal into the engine's furnace – 'We'll need it for these upgradients later', he had said.

The train had no trouble making the incline within the first tunnel, and puffed through the second reasonably well. Then it emerged on to a snaky viaduct about 25 yards long which fed into a forest-girt S-curve tunnel, the Galleria delle Armi, two miles long. At this disaster-point no-one can be 100 per cent sure what happened. It has been reasoned that the man at the throttle was worried by the high reading on his furnace-pressure gauge which apparently did not correspond with the engine speed, and the train must have been slowing badly in the damp narrow tunnel with its steep incline.

When all the cars, except the caboose, had entered the underground passageway, the 8017 groaned to a standstill under the excess weight on icy rails. Meanwhile, in the caboose brakeman Michele Palo was trying to keep himself warm; the engineer had not pulled the whistle-cord to give warning that anything was amiss so Palo assumed that the train had stopped for a signal of some kind – by no means an unusual event on a railway . . .

Finally he decided to take some action. He forced open a lower window and stuck his head out, but the whole train seemed to be encased in the black hole that bored through the hillside. The brakeman drew on his gloves and swung down from his caboose to find out what was holding things up. He had gone no further than a few yards into the black hole when he realized what had happened.

At once he turned round and ran along the track towards the Balvano

---

Tragedy on the underground

Forty one people died and more than 50 were badly hurt when the 8.37 a.m. Northern Line Tube train from Drayton Park crashed through buffers at Moorgate Station, London, on 28 February 1978, and thundered into the brick wall of a dead-end tunnel. It took rescuers three days to cut their way through the compressed sandwich of twisted metal 200 feet below the City streets, and reach the body of driver Leslie Newson, 58. The 50-foot first carriage of the train was crushed to just a third of its normal length.

Crash in Chicago

Forty five passengers died in a web of tangled steel and 300 more were hurt, many seriously, when a local train which had missed its stop began reversing to the platform at Chicago rail station and was hit from behind by a speeding express. The disaster, on 30 October 1972, was the worst in the history of the American mid-west city.

---

depot two miles away downhill. He hoped to arrive in about an hour and get help for some of those aboard 8017. But his nightmare jog-trot took him much, much longer than that – most of the time he found himself forced down on hands and knees. It was 2.50 a.m. when he came within sight of Balvano – at about the same time as Salonia had boarded the engine and started it up. Palo swung his red lantern from the mouth of the Balvano tunnel and yelled: 'Up the track!' 'Up the track!' When Salonia reached Palo he had collapsed on the line, and was moaning '*Sono tutti morti!*' ('They're all dead!')

Salonia had heard no crash, saw no evidence of an accident. Could the 8017 have left the rails? Not possible, Salonia decided, or some noise would have been heard in that snow-hushed countryside. He concluded that Palo had taken leave of his senses – the man was sobbing bitterly and every now and then buried his face in Salonia's jacket. Salonia picked the distraught railwayman up in his arms and carried him to the station where he was gently coaxed to relate what he could remember.

It was now almost 4.00 a.m. Despite the hour, everyone of importance in the town of Balvano was aroused. Salonia edged the 8025 engine slowly up the track to the tunnel Galleria delle Armi. He stopped the 8025 and, in the early morning mist, he made his way on foot to the last car of the 8017 which was held in the tunnel.

There was no sign of an accident, only an eerie, unnatural silence. Salonia slid open the door of one car and entered, lighting the interior with his lantern. Passengers were seated and sprawled in postures of utter relaxation. They looked as if they were asleep, but they were all dead. In every car Salonia entered, the scene was repeated: not one of the 500 showed the slightest flicker of life. The men in the cab were dead too, the engineer still at his throttle with his head rested on the side of the window-pane.

Salonia broke down, hardly able to bear the evidence of his eyes. He took a grip of himself, undid the brakes and backed the 8017 to the engine of his 8025, hitched the engine to the 8017 caboose, and towed the train of peaceful death back to Balvano. The police took over the macabre duty of carrying out the dead and laying them side by side on the station platform for future identification.

In all, 521 people died in the eeriest railway disaster of the century. The Italian State police had the task of reconstructing what must have happened inside the mountain. The 8017 could not have gone very far into the tunnel before its wheels began to slide. Chief engineer Gigliani could easily have backed the train downhill out of the tunnel and on to the viaduct. Instead he chose to press on in a bid to get over the gradient that impeded the train's forward impetus. The four crewmen in the two locomotive compartments – Gigliani and stoker Barbato in the leading engine, throttler Senatore and foreman Ronga in the second cab – set about scooping coal into the firebox. They worked like men possessed, yet the huge wheels, having lost all grip of the rails, simply spun faster and faster over the slippery track, and the train stayed on the same spot.

As the roaring fires devoured the emergency supply of soft coal, not one of the sweating crewmen realized that the fuel was producing lethal carbon-monoxide gas. The passengers – most of whom were asleep – did not worry because the train had stopped within a mountain. The carbon-monoxide took the lives of the four men in the engines, then worked its deadly way through the lungs of the conductor and 516 passengers.

Police, checking every detail, found that five passengers had not been suffocated by the gas; three were black marketeers who were brought to the station-master's office for medical treatment. Later they disappeared discreetly to avoid the questioning which would certainly have exposed their illegal activities, so they were of no help to the police in tackling the mysteries surrounding the 8017.

One survivor, an olive-oil salesman named Domenico Miele, was to prove of great value. He reported that he had stepped off the train at Balvano to stretch his legs for a few minutes. Finding the cold air too much for him, he took a scarf from his luggage, an action which was to save his life. When the train came to dead stop inside the tunnel, Miele was one of the few who had not dropped off to sleep.

When the carbon-monoxide gas reached him, it started him coughing. Miele wrapped his scarf round his mouth as a filter, got off the train and made an unsteady way out of the tunnel. He did not guess that there was killer gas about because he climbed into the next, and last, coach to find another seat, but only reached the vestibule where he fainted and remained prostrate until he was picked up by two policemen who presumed him dead and carried him off to the improvised mortuary on the Balvano station platform.

As a result of partial gas poisoning Miele's hair (so says the official police report on the tragedy) turned from a rich black colour to a soapy grey.

The other surviving passenger was a small dealer named Luigi Cozzolino, but he suffered such severe brain damage that he did not realize what had happened, not even that his wife and eight-year-old son died on that ill-fated 8017.

Because of wartime censorship only one newspaper was allowed to publish a short official notice about the 'mishap'. All lawsuits were ruled out of order because the Allied Military Government had been technically in charge of Italy's railway system and could not be held accountable in law for a 'wartime accident'.

The London Pea-Soupers (1952)

In the old days, they called them 'pea-soupers' – stifling, blanketing fogs which reduced visibility to barely a few feet and invaded the lungs with damp, polluted air. For days at a time, the smog, thick with fumes from industrial waste, would hang over London. For decades, they had been an unpleasant feature of inner-city life. Half-way through this century, they were all but a thing of the past. . . .

Then, in December, 1952 – still many years before today's strict, anti-pollution rules – the unimaginable happened. In the wake of an influenza epidemic which was sweeping the country and terrible floods which hit many coastal areas, killing more than 300 people, a dense, dark cloud began to envelop the capital. It was more than fog or smog; it was worse than any 'pea-souper'. Within a fortnight, more than 4,000 had died in the worst fog and pollution disaster the world has ever witnessed.

Swirling, chill winds failed to disperse the choking smog which brought the city to a standstill; they merely helped spread the highly concentrated sulphur dioxide fumes that pervaded the fog. Dozens of people were killed in road accidents, but the vast majority perished from lung and pollution-related diseases; victims of a nightmare which combined freak weather conditions with poison waste which for decades had been pumping from the chimneys of industrial sites and factories unchecked.

People of all ages, from infants to old-age-pensioners, became tragic statistics in a death toll which swiftly rocketed to alarming proportions. In adults, those most at risk appeared to be in the over 45 age group. The scale of the disaster is best illustrated by the fact that the combined death toll of the two previous worst fog catastrophes, in Donora and the Meuse Valley, was 84 . . . virtually one-fiftieth of the victims of London, 1952.

An analysis of the tragedy by a leading American research professor, Philip Drinker, revealed that sulphur dioxide levels in the fog were 1.3 parts per million which is much lower than levels accepted in factories at the time, but high enough to affect ordinary human beings. Throughout the city, the grim picture was the same. The old and the infirm and even those previously in good health simply died from the pungent fumes which hung in the mist-filled air.

In desperation, thousands of people stayed shut in their homes as the fog

Above: Brixton market, shrouded in smog. Below: Piccadilly Circus at mid-morning

Year's rainfall falls in one day

**More than 150 people died and another 20,000 were made
homeless when savage thunderstorms hit southern Spain on the
night of Thursday, 18 October 1973. A cold front from the North
Atlantic met warm Mediterranean air flows, and created massive
thunderclouds, 30,000 feet high, which crashed against the Sierra
Nevada range of mountains behind Spain's tourist spots. The
towns of La Rabita, where a year's normal rainfall, 8 inches, fell
in one hour, and Puerto Lumbreras were worst hit, but fruit and
wine crops throughout the provinces of Murcia, Almeria and
Granada were devastated in what the authorities called 'the worst
economic disaster in south-eastern Spain for 35 years.'**

continued to cast a shadow of death across the city, refusing to venture into
the perilous streets where, at times, it was impossible to see inches, let alone
feet, ahead. Transport services and entire industries ground to a halt in the
appalling conditions and, under cover of the pungent fog blanket, thieves
went on a massive crime spree, looting shops and properties of tens of
thousands of pounds.

The British Government was stunned by the disaster. Already, there was
growing concern about pollution and a spiralling increase in associated
diseases such as silicosis, asbestosis and pneumoconiosis. But the tragedy
that fell on London prompted immediate action.

Parliament immediately voted to set up an emergency Atmospheric
Pollution Committee to examine the nature, causes and effects of air
pollution. Given wide-ranging powers, the committee was also to examine
the then almost non-existent anti-pollution controls and propose ways of
tightening them to ensure that disaster on such a scale was never repeated.
The findings of that committee were to lead to legislation still in force today.

One man who saw friends and neighbours die as the killer fog gripped
London, told newspapers at the time: 'There were days during that first
fortnight when you just couldn't see your own hand stretched out in front of
you. At times, the streets were deserted, save for the villains who made rich
pickings. It seemed like the entire city was one giant morgue. If you wanted to
remain safe, you just stayed indoors.' 'It was a nightmare that seemed to last
an eternity. To walk out was foolish – but to venture onto the roads in a car
was suicidal. There were literally hundreds of accidents, some of them fatal.
If you did have to go out, you could almost cut through the air with a knife.
The stench of sulphur was unbelievable; every time you took a breath you
were left gasping or thrown into a convulsive fit of coughing. In every street,

it seemed, there was someone who died, or someone whose friends and relatives had died. Mothers were terrified to go out with their babies. Apart from those who died, the number of people who fell ill – many with severe bronchial complaints – was incalculable. It was like living in a nightmare – you couldn't go anywhere and there was nothing you could do to get rid of the problem. You just had to hope and pray that one morning you would wake up and see the sky again.'

Another fog-bound Londoner who lived through the disaster said later: 'People were dropping like flies. When it was all over I was genuinely surprised that no more than slightly over 4,000 had died. It seemed that the only business in the city which had not come to a complete halt was that of the undertaker. Every street had its share of mourners. Day and night it was just the same; you were a prisoner in your own home, helplessly trapped by the fog. If you did go out, and survived the atmosphere, you would have been in real trouble in the event of an accident. The emergency services were totally unable to cope – they just couldn't find their way to the scenes of accidents or even hope to get there in time to the ones they were informed of.'

Within three weeks, the fog had begun to lift and slowly, very slowly, London life began to return to normal as its inhabitants picked up the pieces. Tens of thousands of pounds was pilfered by looters. A trail of devastation lay strewn across the capital. And more than 4,000 people lay dead . . . victims of the killer fog.

Le Mans
(1955)

Le Mans as we know it is the scene of the world-famous classic motor racing event, the French Grand Prix d'Endurance, a 24-hour non-stop event which has converted this ancient town into a gallic Brands Hatch.

The town-hall is built on the site of a former castle, and the town itself, which lies about 100 miles south-west of Paris, is the seat of a bishopric dating back to the third century A.D. King Henry II of England was born here, and its cathedral houses the tomb of Berengaria of Navarre, wife of England's Richard Coeur de Lion.

Today, Le Mans is synonymous with the best in motor-racing, and it has its own history, of which the most dramatic episode occurred in just a few seconds on Saturday, 11 June 1955. In that instant a Mercedes car, momentarily out of control, rocketed off the track into a part of the crowd of more than a quarter of a million spectators, cut a swathe through them, bounced and then exploded in an incandescent star-burst. In less time than it takes to relate, it killed 82 people and seriously injured more than 100 others.

Shock, frenzy, horror? Certainly, and in full numbing measure – but the officials, with a curious *sang froid*, insisted that the race should continue, complete with its attendant fairground carnival music and amusements, while the police, doctors and ambulancemen gathered the seriously injured, the dead and fragments of the dead, and took them away with speedy efficiency to nearby hospitals and mortuaries.

This particular Le Mans Grand Prix had aroused an enormous amount of international interest. World champion Fangio was competing, and new cars with famous drivers were expected to establish new speed records at, as one newspaper reported, 'a pace never seen here before'. Entrants included Mercedes-Benz of West Germany, the Italian Ferraris and Maseratis, the Gordinis of France, British Jaguars, Aston Martins and so on. It was the days when Fangio, Castelotti and Mike Hawthorn were virtually household names, even among the non-aficianados of the sport.

The weather was sunny and hot, and even though some rain was forecast a carnival atmosphere abounded. It was a kind of Royal Ascot of the internal-combustion engine. In the surrounding fairground and bars business boomed as the race got under way in the late afternoon. Bunched together, the leading cars took the bends at 150 mph, and then Fangio and Hawthorn began to break lap records, building up to an average lap speed of 120 mph – as fast as the fastest of any previous Grand Prix. It was exciting and spellbinding for the first two hours, at which point horror struck like a thunderbolt. One of the Mercedes cars slewed from the track, bounced over the earth safety-bank, rocketed through the massed spectators and finally exploded at a cost of nearly 100 lives, and many injured. Time taken – a matter of two or three seconds.

Precisely how this came about has since been a subject of unending controversy. At the time the contest was running well. The attention of the crowd was centred on Mike Hawthorn in a new D-type Jaguar who was seriously challenging world champion Fangio in his silver Mercedes-Benz. Both had gained a lap on Pierre Levegh, the Frenchman in the Mercedes No. 3 team car. No hazard was evident – the cars were 'all systems go' and the drivers in good trim.

Then Mike Hawthorn began to brake and slow down to pull into his pit on the right so that his co-driver, Londoner Ivor Bueb, could take over. During the subsequent inquiry, and some years later in a letter to *The Times*, Hawthorn was quoted as insisting that he had given the prescribed hand signal in accordance with accepted racing practice. As he slowed and pulled over towards his pit, Levegh's Mercedes came up from behind to pass at around 180 mph. In the resulting swerve the Mercedes touched the rear of a British Austin-Healey driven by Lance Macklin.

All motion is relative. That 'touch' at 180 mph hurled the Austin-Healey into a frantic broadside skid 100 yards long, but it ended safely enough and few paid much attention. All eyes were on Levegh's Mercedes. The car skewed and ran into the six-foot-thick earth safety-bank designed to function as an exterior brake and divert the driver back on to the track. This time, however, the reverse happened. The earth bank seemed to lift the car into a somersault so that it soared rocket-like into the air, somersaulted again before falling among the spectators, bounced once more and finally exploded into white-hot component parts, like shrapnel from an anti-personnel bomb.

Those few moments brought for many the instant eternity of death, including the driver himself whose body, thrown from the disintegrating car, was found dead near the roadside.

The shock was immediate but localized, and it is quite likely that only a tiny proportion of the crowd realized that anything at all had happened. It was, perhaps, to isolate those near the scene of death and destruction – a relatively small area – that the *gendarmes* moved in to set up a human barrier that could be penetrated only by doctors, firemen and professionally qualified helpers to speed up rescue work. For the same reason, perhaps, the

The blazing wreckage of the Mercedes car, driven by Pierre Levegh. Inset: the twisted debris of bodies and cars litter the enclosure

Tanker explodes

A tanker loaded with liquid gas exploded as it was driven along the coast road near Tortosa, Spain. The burning tanker crashed through the perimeter wall of Los Alfaques campsite and flung blazing gas over a quarter-mile radius, incinerating tents, caravans and holidaymakers. The disaster, on 11 June 1978, claimed 180 lives, many of them children.

decision was made at a high level to let the show continue – race, music and amusements.

The media were quickly on the spot and the disaster was soon being reported from every angle by international journalists, radio, television and newsreel men. To call it a field-day would be a misnomer; indeed, some film and television reports were so sickening that astonished producers and film editors, despite their love of the sensational, found themselves obliged to make cuts and fades. Even the printed word had to be moderated in many newspapers.

According to one reporter, 'the engine and back axle of the Mercedes sliced like a razor through the packed spectators. Some were decapitated, and for 100 yards along the straight the scene was like a bloodstained battlefield. Wailing men and women tried frantically to find out whether their friends or relations were among the victims. Women's screams rose above the roar of the cars as they continued round the course.'

A seasoned cameraman commented: 'I've covered wars and just about every type of horror job you can think of, but the stuff I've got here in the can is so appalling that it would make people sick to see it. There are kiddies with their heads sliced off – and their hands still gripping the ice-cream cornets they'd been sucking only seconds before. There was one father, mad with grief, refusing to believe that his son was dead and trying to carry him away to safety . . .'

Bodies lay everywhere. Many died en route to hospital. Ironically, those already dead were grotesquely covered with torn-down advertisement banners. Many had been charred by the fuel-fed flames of the Mercedes, whose engine contained a high proportion of weight-saving magnesium – an element well known for its explosive inflammability. Like an incendiary bomb, it defied the firemen and simply burned itself out.

Two English doctors worked alongside their French colleagues at the death site, although they had gone to Le Mans merely to see the race. With the approach of night came rain and a new crisis. The local hospital at Le

Mans, after carrying out more than 80 transfusions, was rapidly running out of blood supplies. More was needed – much more – and urgently.

For the first time since the tragedy, the fairground music was silenced while doctors used the loudspeaker system to make urgent appeals for blood donors. There was no lack of response. Donors queued at waiting ambulances, then, having given blood, went back to watch the race which was still in progress, or to the funfair stalls which were still open for business.

Overcynical? Who can say? Perhaps it was the emotive reaction of the time, but on the other side of the coin the deliberate continuation of the race and funfair avoided possible chaos and obstruction to the essential rescue work in progress. The effect of a quarter of a million visitors trying to leave the ground at the same time can well be imagined.

The competitors themselves were obliged to drive lap after lap around the floodlit track when all of them wished to withdraw from what had become a fiasco. It was now a race in which there could be no true winner, but the sponsors were divided in their reactions. Mercedes, taking a very firm line, desperately tried to contact the firm's directors at Stuttgart for permission to pull out their cars, but the telephone lines were frantically busy and communication was subject to long delays. In the end the West German Federal Government at Bonn intervened. Although the Le Mans organizers wanted the Germans to continue, at 1.45 a.m. on the Sunday the German team manager, Alfred Neubauer, received authority to flag in his two remaining cars which were running first and third, with Britain's Mike Hawthorn lying between.

The head of Jaguar, Mr William Lyons, also debated the abandonment of the race, but circumstances were rather different; his own son had been killed while driving a Jaguar to watch the race. He said, 'I can imagine nothing further from my son's wishes,' adding, without reference to the Mercedes withdrawal, 'racing in that respect is like flying. The risks are acknowledged and respected. But how can we be other than very grieved when a tragedy of this magnitude shadows the sport?'

The 1955 Le Mans Grand Prix was won, if the word has any meaning in retrospect, by Britain's Mike Hawthorn at an average speed of just over 107 mph. He commented after the event: 'It was the one time in my career I'd have been equally glad to lose.'

Hawthorn was naturally the target for criticism, especially in France, for it was his move into the pit that had triggered the subsequent horror. In press correspondence it was alleged that he had failed to give the requisite hand signal to warn the following drivers of his intended move, and that he had misjudged the distance to his pit, overshooting it by some 80 yards. Both

LE MANS

Macklin and Fangio echoed these criticisms some years later, although Hawthorn had been exonerated in the official inquiry following the disaster. Perhaps only Hawthorn himself knew the full truth, but he was killed a few years later (1959) in an ordinary road accident.

The French Government wasted no time in taking action. First, all motor racing was banned until new safety rules had been agreed and established. Second, after due deliberation, the new proposed safety regulations were put forward for international agreement.

Three main points emerged. The first was a ban on all racing events in which both high- and low-powered cars could compete simultaneously (it had been concluded that the relatively slow speed of Lance Macklin's Austin-Healey, hit by the much faster Mercedes, had been largely responsible for the catastrophe). Secondly, it was recommended that public stands on the course should be moved further away from the track, so reducing, if not totally eliminating, hazards to spectators. Finally, the pits, where cars were fuelled and maintained, should be moved over to a special side track well away from the public stands. These changes were internationally accepted and duly put into effect.

Agadir Earthquake (1960)

To the people of Agadir and to the several thousand tourists enjoying its winter sunshine, 2 March 1960 had been just another day. Now, half an hour to midnight and with a high, bright moon looking down on the drowsy city enveloped in the warm clinging darkness of a Moroccan evening, that day was almost over.

In the big, modern hotels near the sea, the lights were going out one by one. The children, tired from a day's ceaseless activity on the magnificent beaches of golden sand and from the continuous excitement of new sights and sounds, had long been asleep. Many of their elders had followed their example, tired from another day of continual sunshine, of excursions to the four-centuries-old Casbah, and of an orgy of writing 'Having a wonderful time, wish you were here' postcards to less fortunate friends who were combating the chill of winter.

Some, of course, remained very much awake. The popular bar at the huge Saada Hotel, just off the main sea-front, still had its fringe of dedicated drinkers; the card salon of nearby Gauthier's had its nightly collection of bridge players who rarely looked up from their cards or score-sheets to gaze out across the hotel's boasted 'panoramic view of the bay'. Away from the hotel area, some of the tourists were sampling the more dubious pleasures of the mainly Muslim quarter of Talbordj lying to the north-west, where cabarets with a 'native' flavour, including the commercialized exotic dances of old Morocco, had their admiring semi-circles of European patrons. Otherwise the whole city was still.

A casual talking point had been the three earth tremors that had shaken the city during the week, but they had been so slight that they had passed almost unnoticed, although some of those at the Saada bar had wittily suggested that their duty-free drinks had more of a 'kick' than usual.

But those tremors had been a promise of more to come.

At 11.39 p.m. there came a fourth, a shock which lasted for nearly 10 whole seconds – an unusually long time – to become the worst earthquake tremor ever recorded in Morocco. The whole of the city and the surrounding countryside trembled and shook with the immeasurable power of that subterranean movement. That comparatively brief moment of time seemed an eternity to everyone in Agadir that night. To many it seemed like the end of the world. To several thousand it *was* the end of their world.

At 11.40 p.m. the moon illuminated a scene of utter, terrifying chaos. The

AGADIR EARTHQUAKE

Agadir, before the horrifying earthquake

great ultra-modern hotels that had been built to satisfy the demand of the post-war tourist boom had suddenly become grotesque heaps of shapeless, dust-covered rubble. Every street was now littered with great piles of stones, masonry and plaster that had spilled across them, to block nearly every road from the shoreline to Talbordj where, a few moments before, many multi-storied blocks of flats had been silhouetted against the night sky. Now they, too, lay in piles of utter ruin. Only one road to this quarter was still open, and that had a huge gaping crack right across it.

As the rumbling and crashing came to an end, a ghastly screaming and shouting arose which developed into hysterical pandemonium as the survivors began to claw their way free of masonry and stones. Agadir had almost ceased to exist; even the ancient Casbah was destroyed, only a few dazed inhabitants, grey with dust and shock, groped their way from the ruins that had been their homes to stagger, shaking and sobbing, across the high pile of masonry that had formerly been the protecting wall to reach the fresh air and comparative quiet of the countryside.

Helpers search the ruins for bodies

With every line of communication cut, it was some time before news of the extent of the disaster was received in the French naval and air base which was still at Agadir (although France had recognized Morocco as an independent kingdom some four years earlier), but little could be done until dawn except alert other cities throughout the country, asking for urgent aid.

Dawn revealed an almost unbelievable sight. Nearly every hotel had been flattened, while damage in the thickly-populated Talbordj quarter had been as much as 90 per cent and some 80 per cent in the 'new town' nearby. Wherever the rescue teams looked they saw ruins with parked cars now shattered and half-buried with masonry. In some hotels, walls had crumbled away to reveal beds, some still sheltering the bodies of unfortunates who had been crushed in their sleep, hanging precariously and almost obscenely from the parapets of tottering walls, while the terrible screaming and moaning of the trapped or cries for help in a variety of languages rose on all sides.

The airport had escaped damage and was turned into a clearing house for the casualties. Aircraft began to arrive to carry the injured to Marrakesh,

Rabat, and other cities which had escaped the effects of the earthquake, although Mogador, 100 miles to the north, had also suffered some damage from the fringes of the earthquake.

A group of sailors was put to work on what had been the imposing Saada Hotel. They struggled desperately against time, their uniforms dusty and torn, but for the most part they only uncovered the crushed bodies of tourists and hotel staff. Even so, they had some success. One group heard the voice of a child calling for its mother, apparently coming from deep below a huge mound of stones that had previously formed part of the façade of the hotel. They dug down, first with spades and picks and then, more gently, with bare hands, until they came upon the child, miraculously alive, trapped in a slight hollow beneath great stones and beams.

But that was to be one of their few successes, for out of the hotel's guest-list of more than 150, only 20 survived.

There was no electricity to light up darkened holes beneath the rubble that might shield a body and no water to dampen the flames which licked at shattered woodwork. Initially, every effort was devoted to finding and then removing the injured to safety and quickly burying the dead to avoid the risk of infection – always a danger to those living in hot climates. Three thousand men of the Moroccan army were rushed to Agadir and then sent to patrol the whole area where the earthquake had also caused much damage. In the Moorish town of Inezgane, some seven miles away, damage was estimated at 30 per cent of the buildings.

A French naval squadron including an aircraft-carrier arrived off the coast; Dutch and Spanish warships joined it; Britain sent aircraft from Gibraltar to land at Agadir's airport. Soon a fleet of some 80 aircraft was operating a shuttle service to airlift the injured. More than 2,000 people were thus evacuated.

There was a number of British tourists in Agadir's hotels, and all of those who survived had alarming stories to tell. Alan Birtles of Warwickshire, for example, recalled that he and his wife were asleep in bed when there was a frightful rushing noise and a lot of crashing and screaming. It was pitch dark, which made matters worse. He tried the bedside light but the electricity cables had been ruptured. As he and his wife lurched about the

---

Earthquake in Iran

More than 26,000 people died when an earthquake destroyed 40 villages in north-east Iran on 19 September 1978. In one village, Tabas, only 2,000 of the 13,000 residents survived.

Tornado destroys Navy

One of the American Navy's greatest losses during World War II was inflicted not by the Japanese, but by the weather. On the evening of 17 December 1944, destroyers, cruisers and aircraft carriers of the Third Fleet Task Force 38 were replenishing stocks of food, fuel and ammunition during a sea rendezvous with support ships when a savage tornado struck the Philippine Sea. One of the commanders said later: 'My ship was riding as though caught in some giant washing machine. We were rolling between heaving cliffs of water, caught in so strong a vice of wind and sea that our 50,000 horse-power engines were helpless.' It was nine hours before he regained control of his ship, after the fleet had bobbed like helpless shuttlecocks, unable to prevent collisions in the sledgehammer waves. A total of 790 officers and men were lost overboard, killed at their stations or went down with their ships. Eighty more were badly hurt. Three destroyers were lost, five other ships had suffered major damage, and 146 aircraft were either lost or unflyable. Admiral Chester Nimitz, commander-in-chief of the Pacific Fleet, said: 'It is the greatest loss we have taken in the Pacific without compensatory return since the first Battle of Savo.'

room they found that the earthquake had brought all the drawers tumbling from the furniture, and they soon realized that the plaster from the ceiling overhead was still falling about them. He managed to find a cigarette-lighter and by its meagre light they struggled into some clothes. Then, going to the door, they found it had jammed and they had to break it down before they could escape. 'We broke down the doors of other rooms in the corridor to help people out', he concluded.

Richard Waddington who had been staying at the Marhaba Hotel, one of the few large buildings that had not collapsed completely, stated that the most awful thing about the disaster was 'the terrible screaming and shouting from people trapped under the rubble; but you could not do anything about it.' He went on: 'I was fortunate, I suppose, because I was under only six feet of rubble and they got me out in six hours. My father was 16 feet down. It took 22 hours to free him. My mother was farther down still. She was dead when they got to her.'

At the end of that first day the authorities ordered the complete evacuation of Agadir, then sealed off the whole area except for essential services. The Crown Prince of Morocco held a Press Conference to announce that the death-roll had risen to 10,000. That figure included 4,000 dead already

AGADIR EARTHQUAKE

One of the badly damaged buildings in Agadir

found, with an estimated 6,000 still buried beneath the ruins. Some 20,000 people had escaped unhurt, he said, and the 2,000 injured had already been evacuated. Final figures were never accurately established, and other sources quoted widely differing statistics.

The rescue work went on, although by now it had developed into a search for bodies. So much quicklime had been scattered about to prevent infection that one observer said that parts of the city resembled snow-covered fields.

Yet there were miraculous survivals. On 9 March, a week after the earthquake, three Moroccans were rescued quite unscathed. A father and his 10-year-old son had been dug out alive and rescue workers began to search around the same area until, led by weak cries, they found another man. On the following day, eight more were rescued. Rescue workers listening and calling among the débris were answered by feeble cries on 11 March and during that day they dug out a man of 24, three women and a family of three Jewish children, two girls and a boy of six. The following day two more were rescued, one a 28-year-old Muslim, the other, as it happened, the father of the three children rescued the previous day. The two girls, Alice and Jacqueline Kalfon, related how they had told stories and sung to their little brother Armand during their ordeal beneath the débris of their house. All were rushed to hospital, where Armand died a few hours later.

Rescue work was also going on in the remote areas of the Atlas Mountains where nearly 600 were reported dead and more than 2,000 homeless.

Helicopters circling over the devastated areas reported that in some instances the ground had opened like giant jaws and swallowed villagers 'by the dozen'.

The earthquake had a strange effect upon the Atlantic coastline and seabed which made an extensive hydrographic survey essential. At one place where the water had been charted at 1,200 feet, soundings showed that it was now only 45 feet. This was not only inshore; for nine miles from the coastline soundings showed a depth of 1,200 feet instead of the previous 4,500 feet.

The Vaiont Dam (1963)

In the north-eastern corner of Italy, where the Italian Alps merge with those of Switzerland and Jugoslavia, there are many rivers which are the source of water and hydro-electric power for northern Italy. Across the valleys dams have been built and reservoirs created.

The Vaiont Dam formed part of a complex of five dams, which together made up the north-west-Piave hydro-electric scheme. When it was opened in 1960 it was the third highest concrete dam in the world, its wedge-shaped wall towering 873 feet above the Piave river and the valley below. In this valley, on the banks of the river, lay a number of small villages. Closest to the dam was Longarone, a village of less than 2,000 people, and a number of outlying hamlets.

The autumn of 1963 was unusually wet. Rain had loosened the rocks and earth of the mountain slopes which formed the shores of the reservoir. One of these, Mount Toc, which rises steeply to a height of 6,000 feet, had caused such apprehension that on 8 October a mayor in the district issued a warning to fishermen and others who might venture on the lake shores of the possibility of landslides causing dangerous waves.

Anybody who lives close to a dam is aware of the possibility of a fault and the disaster that could follow. The people in the district of Longarone were no exception, but they had no apprehension of danger on the night of Wednesday, 9 October 1963. At 11.00 p.m. they were all at home, either in bed or watching television. Fifteen minutes later a vast avalanche swept down the slopes of Mount Toc and thousands of tons of rocks, mud, earth and uprooted trees tumbled into the lake. The effect was that of throwing a large stone into a basin of water. Although the reservoir was by no means full it promptly overflowed, spilling over the top of the dam and pouring into the valley below.

The few survivors said later they heard that fearful sound which is so often described as the first intimation of disaster – a noise like thunder. They assumed at once that the dam had given way and, pausing only to gather up those nearest to them, they fled, but only the people whose houses lay close to the high ground at the edge of the valley had any chance. Over the lip of the dam poured a torrent of water, mud, rock and timber, creating a towering wall which swept along the valley below, swirled up the hillside and engulfed villages in a horrifying, overwhelming tide.

The natural assumption that both survivors and the authorities initially

One of the many victims of the collapse of the Vaiont Dam

Eight villages destroyed

For days, the 30,000 inhabitants of the Peruvian city of Huaraz
had basked in scorching sunshine, with the temperature reaching
84°F. But on Saturday, 13 December 1941, that sunshine cost 7,000
of them their lives. At 6.45 that morning, the tongue of a glacier
on snowcapped Mount Palcaraju, towering 20,575 feet above the
town, snapped off and crashed into one of the two catchment lakes
below. It was already full with ice melted over the previous days.
Tons of displaced water fell into the second, lower lake, which
breeched its natural moraine dam with a hideous explosion. Eight
villages were obliterated as a 50-foot wall of water crushed houses
like cardboard cartons. Then the flood careered through Huaraz,
disintegrating everything in its path, before plunging onwards,
carving a 135-mile path of destruction until it roared into the
Pacific at Chimbote.

---

made – that the dam had burst – was not corrected until the dawn. The night had been chaos and pandemonium: the sun rose to reveal a macabre scene – a vast, silent desert of rock and mud and rubble, with here and there the remains of a building. Longarone, four-fifths destroyed, was a heap of stones; so were the nearby hamlets of Faè and Pirago, where all the inhabitants died. Two other hamlets, Codissago and Castellavazzo, lost half their population; the two on the lake were wiped out, with three-quarters of the population missing.

It took time to establish these facts, for communications were destroyed. Telephone and telegraph lines were cut; railway lines turned and twisted in crazy spirals of buckled steel; and roads leading into the devastated villages were unidentifiable swamps. When the Italian Minister of Public Works visited the scene he described it as 'a truly biblical disaster . . . like Pompeii before the excavations began.'

With daylight came the first of the helpers, ploughing through the morass in the valley below the dam, where the river was swollen to twice its natural size by the waters pouring into it. Throughout the day bodies were washed up as workers struggled to reach the stricken villages in a frantic search for survivors. The final approaches to Longarone, now quagmires blocked with rubble and timber and the bodies of dead cattle, became choked with soldiers, ambulances, lorries and people desperately hoping for news of friends or relatives.

There was little hope for those who had not managed to escape to the high ground. The force of the great wave could be seen in the twisted pieces of metal, the total destruction, the bodies found hurled high into trees. The problem of extricating the bodies was immense: the municipal authorities at Belluno immediately ordered 500 coffins but as the days passed it became apparent that these would not be enough. Five days later rescuers were still digging for bodies and the problems of identification grew. Many were disfigured and denuded of clothing: whole families had died and there was nobody left to identify them. Eventually many were buried, unknown, although occasionally one of the thousands of helpers would find himself facing and able to identify someone he once knew.

The gruesome task was soon well organized. Bodies were extracted, sprayed with disinfectant, put in plastic shrouds and into simple coffins away from the warm sun as quickly as possible. A helicopter service was established and bodies arrived heaped on lorries, or carried, roughly-covered, on stretchers from the helicopters. The final death-toll totalled 1,189, although possibly some were not found. But on the morning of 12 October, two children were discovered, still alive, in the cellar under the débris of their home. While there was still hope of survivors, the rescue work continued at full intensity.

An urgent inquiry was made into the safety of the dam. It was inspected and found to have suffered only some damage to the top of its retaining wall. The vast extent of the landslide could be judged from the fact that little over a third of the original reservoir remained. Instead, a new mountain filled the centre of the dam, some grass and lopsided trees still covering its surface.

Almost immediately the cause of the disaster became a political issue and

Dam collapses

Uneasy residents had tried in vain to block the building of the Teton Dam in eastern Idaho, 50 miles from Yellowstone Park. They feared the structure, taller than a 30-storey building, would be undermined by channels, caverns and fissures in the volcanic rock of the canyon walls at each side. At 11.57 a.m. on 5 June 1976, their worst fears were realized. Erosion on the north side of the dam started the structure crumbling, and the crushing weight of 275 million tons of water plunged through the cavity created, sending a 100-foot wall of water cascading towards the small towns in the flood plain. More than 2,500 homes were destroyed, 17,000 head of livestock drowned, 100,000 acres of farmland were buried by sand and gravel silt, and property damage totalled £200,000,000. More than 2,000 people were hurt, but miraculously only 11 died. Had the dam broken at night, said Governor Cecil Andrus, thousands would have been lost.

THE VAIONT DAM

Above: soldiers search the Piove River for bodies

Left: Victims were buried in enormous mass graves

Thames floods

The River Thames and its estuary broke its banks on 31 January 1953, flooding large areas of Kent and Essex. The death toll was 307. There was also extensive flooding of the Continental coast, particularly in Holland, raising the total of dead to more than 2,000.

the subject of exhaustive inquiries. Rock-falls and small earth movements of the mountain were known to have occurred. The crucial question was: should a dam have been built in that situation in the first place? Three years after its completion it came to light that research was still being made into the suitability of its location.

A court of inquiry was set up to consider a number of questions and to establish whether the disaster could have been avoided. It had to consider various aspects: Was the location badly chosen? Was the dam badly designed? Was the area, and in particular the hazard constituted by the mountain, monitored frequently enough? Had the local authorities taken sufficient care in the warnings they issued? A minor earth tremor had been recorded in the mountain about half an hour before the landslide occurred. It was stated that the strength of the seismic waves showed that strain had been building up inside the mountain for some time. Could the people have been warned in time of the possibility of an earth-fall?

Although the court had been involved as a result of Communist pressure upon the Government whom they accused of negligence, it soon became apparent that there were grounds for such an inquiry; when its findings were eventually published there seemed little doubt that, with more care and more exhaustive enquiries into its potential dangers, the site would never have been chosen. The nationalized Italian electricity industry, which was responsible for the hydro-electric scheme, was found to be at fault. Builders and civil engineers were also found to carry some of the blame for a

One million people dead in Pakistan

The most devastating cyclone and tidal wave ever recorded hit east Pakistan on 12 and 13 November 1970. The final death toll, announced after the country became Bangladesh in December 1971, was over one million, and more than half the 1.4 million population of four islands, Bhola, Charjabbar, Hatia and Ramagati, was wiped out.

construction unsuitable to its particular site. It was common knowledge that there had been concern over the safety of the mountain. When the dam was being built and the reservoir filled, a series of landslides and cracks had appeared in the mountain, which had had to be reinforced with concrete to a depth of several feet on either side of the dam. Instruments recorded stresses and strains on the rock face, and the reservoir was not completely filled until two years after the dam had been completed. At the time of the flood all the men working at the dam were killed, but one who had worked on the original construction claimed that the technicians were waiting for such a disaster from one day to the next.

The local authorities, said the inquiry, must have known of this situation. Why did they do no more than warn the local inhabitants of the dangers on the lake itself? Some communities living around the lake and on Mount Toc had been evacuated. Should not the inhabitants of the valley also have been evacuated? Or at least warned of the possible dangers in strong terms?

As a direct result of the inquiry, the ill-conceived Vaiont Dam was closed down. The devastated villages were rebuilt and new factories sited in the valley.

The Florence Floods (1966)

In the late autumn of 1966 exceptionally severe weather with gales and frequent cloud-bursts struck almost the whole of Europe, raging for several days from Poland across Germany to the shores of the North Sea, down the coast into Holland and across France and Switzerland. In these areas the storms led to some loss of life, considerable damage and great inconvenience. But in Italy they spawned a disaster.

Because of its physical features many parts of Italy have always been subject to heavy flooding. As distinct from Britain, for instance, where the source of most rivers is only slightly above downstream areas, in Italy they rise in many cases thousands of feet above the plains, in the Western Alps, in the Dolomites to the north-east, and in the Apennines, the central ridge which runs like a backbone down the peninsula. In times of heavy rainfall these rivers, reinforced from innumerable mountain streams, pour down at tremendous speed, bringing with them masses of rock and other débris, particularly in the Dolomites where the higher slopes are very unstable. Certain precautions can be taken, of course, dredging river beds, building up banks, but there are times when Nature mocks these efforts.

Such was the case in 1966. Winds rising sometimes to hurricane force swept through the whole length of Italy and brought with them rains of an enormous intensity. It was as though, after weeks of intermittent rain, the sky had suddenly become an ocean which was now falling in a solid mass on the land.

The deluge lasted for two days and in some places, notably the Dolomites, six months' average rainfall came down in 24 hours. This alone would have flooded the northern plains to a depth of several feet, but at least the water would have been fairly stagnant. However, a swirling, destructive tide was created by the rivers swollen yet further by snow melted by warm mountain winds, which burst their banks and roared down at terrifying speed, sweeping aside great stretches of forest that lay in their path and carrying with them an ever-increasing load of rock and débris.

In Friuli-Venezia-Giulia, the north-eastern province at the head of the Adriatic, scores of farms with all their livestock were overwhelmed by floods, avalanches, mud-slides and giant boulders, while in many villages and towns, Trento, for instance, Merano and Bressanone, the streets were submerged in mud to a depth which swallowed up cars and buses. Long sections of road surfaces were completely carried away, railway lines were

---

Town disappears in liquid landslide

The earth literally opened up and swallowed a town in Canada in 1971. Saint-Jean-Vianney was a prosperous, well-kept community of 1,308 people, 135 miles north of Quebec. But it was built on treacherous soil – soluble clay with pockets of sand. On the grey, rainy evening of 4 May, the saturated pockets of sand started liquifying the clay, and quickly a brown river, 60 feet deep, began to flow as the soil vanished to a depth of 100 feet. Homes and people were sucked into the liquid landslide. When the clay began to solidify again, at midnight, 31 men, women and children had vanished for ever, and 38 houses had disappeared. Survivors were resettled in near-by Arvida, and Saint-Jean-Vianney was wiped off all maps.

---

cut, bridges demolished and so much wreckage was deposited in river beds that their level in some places rose many feet above roads running alongside.

For a while the north-east provinces were completely cut off except by radio, and an exhausted messenger who reached Venice over mountain tracks from the Dolomites was regarded as a curiosity. He said: 'For days we have been fighting against the fury of rivers without ceasing.'

One third of Italy was stricken by floods which Interior Minister Taviani described as the worst in history. The Po valley was flooded from both ends, by the overflowing river and by salt water when raging seas broke through dykes protecting the delta. Here one third of the population had to be evacuated, including 12,000 from the island of Donzella lying between two branches of the river.

In Venice sea and sky together produced the worst floods in a thousand years, the main danger coming from the sea. The fate of the city still depended on a system of dykes more than 400 years old which linked the islands separating the Lagoon from the Adriatic. Their upkeep had been neglected, especially during World War II, and early in November exceptionally rough seas combined with gales broke through a section of dyke at the island of Pellestrina. Immediately a wall of water poured into the city, rising to a height of seven feet in some streets and five feet in St Mark's Square, including the cathedral. For 48 hours, until repairs could be carried out and the flood began to subside, life was completely paralyzed.

The London *Times* correspondent reported that Venice was like a gigantic, half-sunken boat. He should have said 'a torpedoed tanker'. Oil storage tanks used for central heating had burst spreading slicks over the flood, and it was this oil-scummed water that ruined the stocks of 4,000

A wrecked car in a Florence Piazza

THE FLORENCE FLOODS

Clearing up after the flood

shops, an immense amount of private property and the ground-floor contents of half the city's hotels. Fortunately there was little damage to art treasures. If the gale had continued for only a few more hours, however, the city centre with its magnificent heritage would have been destroyed. Even so, the damage caused was astronomical.

The shops could be restocked, but it would not be so easy to restore agriculture. Before the war, the fertile area of Tuscany known as the Maremma had been largely marshland infested by malaria. Much of it had been reclaimed and the malaria eradicated, and a thriving industry started based on dairy farming and the production of fruit and vegetables for export. All this was ruined by the floods which submerged four-fifths of the town of Grosetto lying at the centre of the area, 80 per cent of the livestock was destroyed and damage caused exceeded that in the entire province of Venezia.

The heaviest cultural blow was struck at Florence and this aspect of Italy's disaster above all others caught the horrified imagination of the world. Cradle of the Italian Renaissance, a major shrine of western civilization, with its palaces, magnificent Romanesque buildings, and 40 museums housing many of the world's greatest art treasures, Florence was to suffer the fate of Venice – and worse.

On 4 November, the River Arno traversing the oldest part of the city burst its banks. Normally a man running can keep pace with the fastest flowing river, but on this day the Arno in a huge ungovernable flood surged forward at 40 miles an hour (a film made on the spot shows a car being hurled down the Via Formabuoni at just this speed). For several hours the torrent poured through the city spreading ever wider, flooding buildings and rising in places, including the Cathedral Square and the famous eleventh-century Baptistry, to over 15 feet. The best that anyone could do was to save a few possessions and escape drowning. Twenty-four hours later the deluge began to abate, leaving behind a massive residue of glutinous yellow mud, and in the following days it was possible to start surveying the damage. Final estimates showed 17 people dead, 45,000 homeless (a tenth of the population), 40,000 cars wrecked as well as 18,000 shops, including the workshops of some of the goldsmiths and leather-workers for which Florence was famous.

The loss and damage were enormous. Again, oil from burst tanks, and in some places naphtha, mixed with the flood and added to its destructiveness. Many famous buildings were swamped, among them the Medici Chapel, the San Firenzi Palace, the Casa di Dante, the Capella del Pazzi at Santa Croce and the church of Santa Maria Novella. Six hundred paintings by well-known masters were under water for hours when the basement of the famous

Horrific dam-burst

The world's worst dam-burst disaster happened in Morvi, Gujarat, India, on 11 August 1979. More than 5,000 people perished when the Manchhu River dam gave way.

Uffizi Gallery was flooded. Totally destroyed at the same time were 130,000 photographic negatives of Florentine art, many of them irreplaceable.

Elsewhere in the city there were other heavy casualties: the entire State Records of Tuscany from the fourteenth century to 1860, nineteenth-century newspaper files – a loss now making a detailed history of the Risorgimento impossible, Etruscan collections in the Archaeological Museum, the musical scores of Scarlatti, the private papers of Amerigo Vespucci (the Italian explorer who gave his name to America) and the earliest painting in Western art, the 'Cruxifixion' by Cimabue (1240–1302).

Worst hit of all were the libraries. For days more than 6,000,000 volumes, a great many of them unique, lay submerged under water and murky sludge in the State Archives and the vaults of the Biblioteca Nazionale, the equivalent of the British Museum Library – a potential loss which would have had a shattering effect on every aspect of future study and research. At once, a massive international rescue operation was set in motion, with experts from all over Europe coming to advise and help. Even so, the restoration, wherever possible, of these works and the paintings was to take years. Owing to the dissolvance of glue used in bindings and size in the paper, many books when salvaged were as solid as bricks. Each volume had to be cleaned, dried, treated with chemicals to prevent fungus and the pages cautiously prised apart. Finally each volume had to be rebound.

Every job of restoration had to be done as soon as possible to avoid rapid deterioration and speed was achieved by giving crash courses to teams of students and then putting them under the supervision of a single expert. All

Sacred mountain explodes

The Indonesian island paradise of Bali was plunged into hellish nightmare in April 1964 when Gunung Agung, regarded by natives as their holiest mountain, blew its volcanic cone. More than 1,500 people died and 87,000 were made homeless by choking ash from the 10,309 feet peak.

this caught the attention of the outside world, but naturally the people involved in the 36,000 square miles of Italy that had been devastated were more interested in obtaining credit to get on their feet again. There had been damage in 800 municipalities; 22,000 farms and private homes had suffered; 50,000 animals had been lost, thousands of tractors made useless. Total damage was estimated at £575 million ($1,090 million). The death-toll in all Italy was 112.

In Florence, a fortnight after the disaster, the people were working hard to succour the homeless, start business again and clean up their beautiful city. They were not relying much on government help; they knew official red tape too well. Enthusiasm bursting through his sober prose, the London *Times* correspondent noted: 'Tuscan sturdiness has risen above the ruin of the city's delicate grace.' He noticed an interesting point: it was the 'beatniks', so criticized by their elders as useless drop-outs, who were flinging themselves into relief work with the most astonishing energy. 'Beatniks', he added, 'are better than bureaucrats.'

A year later the people were back in their homes and at work again. Museums, galleries and libraries had re-opened and it was said that: 'The golden city of the Renaissance glitters again.' But despite intensive work on the river-bed and its banks, and the organization of a flood early-warning system, anxiety must remain. Asked what would happen if it rained like *that* again, a city official replied: 'We must just hope that it won't.'

Astronauts and Cosmonauts (1967 and 1971)

It was the disaster which had to happen.

Until 27 January 1967, the safest form of transport known to man had been the space capsule. Dozens of American astronauts and Soviet cosmonauts had ridden into space in giant rockets, fuelled by an explosive mixture of liquid oxygen and hydrogen. They had spun around the earth, covering millions of miles. They had walked in space with only the thin layers of the fabric of their pressurized suits separating them from instant death. They had ridden back to earth in the fireballs of their capsules, splashing down in oceans with pinpoint accuracy.

Their space machines were seemingly infallible, a technological marvel of new metals and electronic circuitry which had come straight from a designer's drawing board.

They were pushing science through new barriers every day and they boasted their biggest fear was running the same risk as a weekend amateur skydiver, that the simple technology of a nylon parachute would fail them on the last few thousand feet of their return to earth.

No effort of technical talent or expense had been spared to make America's space exploration programme statistically safer than driving on the nation's freeways in the rush hour. There had not been a single fatality in space, although ironically three of America's astronauts had died in the past year in off-duty plane crashes.

The crew of the Apollo One spacecraft, Virgil 'Gus' Grissom, Ed White and Roger Chaffee, were highly skilled fliers and supremely confident members of the National Aeronautics and Space Administration astronaut corps. They were members of the Apollo project to place the first men safely on the moon.

All three men were requested to report for duty on Launch Pad 34 of the Kennedy Space Center near Cocoa Beach, Florida, for yet another series of tedious rehearsals inside their cramped command module. They would spend a whole day in their space suits, strapped uncomfortably lying on their backs in the capsule, repeating over and over again the routine of cockpit drill. The thrill of the thundering acceleration of lift-off was not due for another month.

For five repetitive hours they ran through the drill. Gus Grissom, a 40-year-old Air Force pilot, a Korean war ace and veteran of two previous space missions, called out the crisp responses to the ground control's requests for the information displayed on his control console computer and instrumental panel.

A ground control technician was first to notice the malfunction. His television monitor, linked to a camera inside the Apollo capsule suddenly flashed pure white and then darkened. Puzzled, he leaned over to adjust the brightness and contrast controls.

As he did so, an anguished voice screeched through the ground control loudspeakers and headphones: 'Fire . . . I smell fire . . .' There were three seconds of silence then the voice of Ed White: 'Fire in the cockpit . . .'

Tape recorders in ground control picked up seven seconds of 'clawing and pounding to open the hatch' then the voice of Roger Chaffee pleading: 'We're on fire . . . get us out of here . . .'

Then there was silence.

In just four minutes an emergency crew had sprinted from the ground level concrete blast-proof control room and reached the top of the gantry by high-speed elevator. Their hands blistering from the scorching surface of the capsule, two of them wrenched open the main hatch. It was already too late. The crew of Apollo One were dead. They had been killed in a matter of seconds, sprawled lifeless in their take-off positions, on top of a three stage empty rocket, perched motionless just 218 feet off the ground.

The world had suffered its first space exploration disaster, right here on earth.

The leading members of the rescue squad began to reel back from the hatch, blinded by smoke, choking and inhaling searing gases from the oxygen rich blast of flame which roared from the twisted hatch. Their pure white overalls blackened and charred, the emergency team were forced to retreat along the catwalk from the gantry.

In the control room at ground level the pictures on the television cameras cleared as the swirling black smoke billowed out of the moon-ship. The bodies of the three astronauts were clearly visible, killed almost instantly by the ferocity of the inferno, their heat resistant space suits smouldering. As all external power supplies to Apollo One were cut off, the launch control director Dr Kurt Debus ordered the emergency teams: 'Stay away from the capsule. There is nothing you can do for them now.'

For the next six hours the unblinking eye of the television camera and its wide angle lens impassively relayed the scene of the horror to the control room as the bodies of the astronauts remained strapped in their seats. Few of the men in the control room could bring themselves to look.

ASTRONAUTS AND COSMONAUTS

At midnight, under the cold glare of floodlights, the medical teams, many of them with tears in their eyes, gently lifted the three bodies from the gutted remains of Apollo One.

Then began the inquest to find out what had caused the fatal spark which had turned the rich, life-giving oxygen of the space capsule into a killer gas, fuelling a tiny flame into a roaring holocaust within seconds. Experts began to recall that there had been several previous warnings of the potentially fatal risks of using pure oxygen in the NASA space vehicles.

Oxygen is the gas in our atmosphere which allows us to breathe, and allows burning to take place. It makes up only about one-fifth of our air. The remaining four-fifths is mainly nitrogen, unbreathable and not capable of supporting a flame.

The Soviet space technicians who designed the cosmonaut carrying Soyuz

Virgil Grissom, Edward White and Roger Chaffee during their Apollo Project training

Cable car plummets

Forty two people died when a cable car plunged to earth at the north Italian ski resort of Cavalese on 9 March 1976.

space capsules, boosted into their orbit by truly awesome rocket power, preferred to use a cumbersome but safe oxygen and nitrogen gas mixture. They knew that they could save precious payload weight by using pure oxygen, but the sheer power of their rockets gave them an enormous advantage over their American rivals.

The oxygen-nitrogen mixing system was weighty but simple technology.

The American space programme controllers had to concede that even their mighty Saturn rockets could not match the brute power of the Soviet boosters. They had been set a challenge by the late President John F. Kennedy after whom their space centre was named. America's prestige as the world's most technologically advanced nation had been severely dented in the early days of the 'space race' as the Soviets piled up one pioneering space achievement after another. The President's challenge had been to put a man on the moon and return him safely to earth before the decade of the Sixties ended.

To meet that deadline NASA had to squeeze every ounce of power from their rocket boosters and save every possible ounce of weight in the capsules and command modules which were to be lifted into space. So they chose an atmosphere of pure oxygen inside the Apollo capsules, dispensing with the need for heavy mixing equipment and bulky nitrogen cylinders. Soviet technology, many NASA scientists explained, could throw iron-clad monster spaceships into orbit. The Americans would close the gap in the space race with the superior sophistication of their machines.

But many worried experts in the U.S. space programme had warned of the risks of using an oxygen-rich atmosphere in space cabins. Only two years before the Apollo One disaster, NASA's chief medical adviser Dr. Randolph Lovelace had handed the Agency a grim report on 'the potential dangers of 100 per cent oxygen atmosphere'.

Dr Lovelace reported that in one incident in a space cabin being tested inside an aircraft at 33,000 feet, a tube in a television monitor had overheated, causing hot plastic to drip on to a control panel. The crew were alerted by the fumes. 'Instead of focussing attention on the hazards of fire', he claimed, 'this accident gave a false sense of security.' A second fire had broken out inside a spaceship simulator at Brooks Air Force Base in Texas.

Two crewmen in space suits were practising a mission when one spotted a glow from behind an instrument panel. Within seconds part of the panel had burst into flames. The cause of the fire was never discovered.

The most dangerous fire had happened at the Naval Air Center in Philadelphia in a chamber containing pure oxygen at only one-third of the pressure of the Apollo capsule. A light bulb in the chamber burned out and a crewman replacing it caused a tiny spark as he screwed a new bulb into the socket. In the instantaneous flash fire which followed, the clothing of the four men inside the chamber immediately caught fire and they were all severely burned.

But other scientists at the Manned Spacecraft Center in Houston, Texas, came up with the comforting re-assurance that, even in a pure oxygen atmosphere, a fire in a spacecraft would simply smother itself – if it was orbiting in space. A fire spread, they explained, because a current of oxygen keeps it fed. The oxygen heated by the flame becomes lighter and rises up, letting fresh, cold oxygen in to keep the fire spreading. But in space there is no gravity, no up and no down. The burnt out oxygen would not rise, it would choke the flames.

Apollo One commander Gus Grissom certainly knew and accepted the risks of being a spaceman. He had only recently attended a hearing of the U.S. Congressional Space Committee with fellow astronaut John Glenn. Grissom had nodded his agreement when Glenn had told the Congressmen: 'You may as well realise now that some future space flight will fail, probably with the loss of life. There will be failures, there will be sacrifices, there will be times when we are not riding on such a crest of happiness as we are now.'

Grissom, the spaceman who was to die in a simple rehearsal in an earth-bound rocket, had been strongly tipped for captaincy of the first flight to the moon.

He had made two previous flights into orbit and had faced death on his first space mission – he almost drowned. His complex Mercury space capsule had performed perfectly in orbit but on splashdown in the Pacific his escape hatch had accidentally jettisoned. Grissom, weighed down by his bulky space suit, had to be rescued by NASA scuba divers as the capsule, the Liberty Bell 7, filled with water and sank.

Elevator tragedy

The world's worst elevator disaster happened at Vaal Reefs gold mine in South Africa on 27 March 1980. The cage plunged 1.2 miles down the liftshaft, killing all 23 passengers.

Major Ed White, 36, had been the second American to walk in space when he stepped out of his Gemini Four spacecraft 150 miles above the Gulf of Mexico and drifted alongside the capsule for fourteen minutes.

He said prophetically after that flight: 'As we fly more and more spacecraft we are going to have one come down and probably going to lose somebody. But I wouldn't want that to hold up the space programme.'

Roger Chaffee, 31, a navy lieutenant commander, was the new boy to the astronaut trio, eager for his first taste of space adventure.

The probable cause of the fire which killed Gus Grissom, Ed White and Roger Chaffee was a loose wire which would have sparked harmlessly behind the control panel but which turned into the fuse of an atmospheric firebomb in the rich oxygen of their cabin.

The Apollo One disaster set the U.S. manned space programme back by 18 months, until the capsule interior was re-designed with spark-proof electrical insulation and a new quick release which could easily be opened by astronauts from the inside.

On 19 April 1971 the permanent space station, Salyut One was launched into orbit. It was thrust into space by the Proton booster rocket, Russia's most powerful. The Soyuz Ten capsule docked with Salyut a few days later but technical problems with the airlock prevented the crew boarding the orbiting station.

On 6 June, a successful docking was made by Soyuz Eleven and its three cosmonauts, Georgi Dobrovolsky, 43, the commander, Viktor Patsayev, 38, a test engineer and Vladislav Volkov, 35, the flight engineer.

The three jubilant cosmonauts spent a record 23 days aboard Salyut while in ground control anxious Soviet doctors monitored the medical condition of the men. They were concerned as to what prolonged weightlessness would do to their physical condition. Within ten days the men had weakened alarmingly, losing much of their muscle power as they floated through space.

Without the force of gravity to make them expend energy, their muscles became flabby. But that was no great problem. In the zero gravity of space the cosmonauts had no difficulty in moving bulky telescope and camera equipment with their fingertips and performing amazing feats of 'weight lifting'.

Patsayev, the test engineer, even busied himself planting seedlings in the space station for mankind's first space garden.

On 30 June, after a flawless space mission, Commander Dobrovolsky disengaged his Soyuz from the space station and fired his retro-rockets for precisely two and a half minutes to start the slow, controlled descent to earth.

In the ground control room the medical specialists began to fuss over their three record-breaking men, warning them by radio not to try to leave their capsule on landing because they would not have the strength to stand on their own two feet. They would have to be carried out like babies until the muscle power returned to their limbs. Floating effortlessly in space, Dobrovolsky laughed: 'We will just sit back and let you do all the work.'

As the craft seared its way back to earth, radio contact was lost, a routine breakdown of radio signals caused by the violent heat and static electricity experienced by all spacecraft burning their way back through the earth's atmosphere.

At 23,000 feet, the recovery parachutes blossomed open and Soyuz drifted towards the ground. Twenty feet above the soil of Kazakhstan, powerful rockets gave one final braking blast and Soyuz made a feather-light touchdown. The recovery crew opened the hatch, ready to lift the returning heroes to the waiting helicopters.

Inside, the three men were dead.

The small explosive bolts which had been detonated in space to separate Soyuz from the Salyut space station had jarred open an air valve in the main hatch. As the capsule began its return to earth, the cosmonauts slowly began to suffocate as their precious air leaked away into the fringes of space.

His reflexes slowed and his muscles wasted by more than three weeks of weightlessness, Commander Dobrovolsky had been too weak to raise his arm against the force of deceleration to close the valve.

Less than six weeks later, the memories of the American astronauts and the Soviet cosmonauts, were commemorated in a fitting tribute. Not just the crews of Apollo One and Soyuz Eleven, but also the spacemen who had died in plane crashes and training missions.

Apollo Fifteen mission commander David Scott had touched down on the surface of the moon on 30 July 1971, just two years after lunar pioneer Neil Armstrong. The most sophisticated part of his equipment was the Lunar Rover, a battery powered car which allowed him and his crewman Jim Irwin to drive for miles over the moon's surface. They drove to the edge of the lunar chasm, the Hadley Rille, overlooking a ridge 1,200 feet high.

There they placed a small metal figure of a fallen spaceman, and a plaque listing in alphabetical order, regardless of nationality, the names of eight astronauts and six cosmonauts who had given their lives for space exploration.

Peru Earthquake (1970)

In those parts of the world which, through faults in the earth's crust, are particularly susceptible to earthquakes, the people learn to live with the risk and to accept it as part of their lives, in the same way that people who live in the northern hemisphere accept the probability of snow in winter.

Peruvians have been aware of the likelihood of earthquakes throughout the centuries (the recorded history of earthquakes in Peru dates back to the Spanish chroniclers of 1619) and have learned to accept them philosophically. Few, however, imagined such a devastating earthquake as the one which occurred on Sunday, 1 May 1970, affecting 600 miles of the Peruvian coast and a vast hinterland, leaving dozens of towns in ruins or totally obliterated, and killing a staggering total of at least 50,000 people.

Peruvians are ardent football fans, and at 3.00 that afternoon most of them had settled down at home to watch the first match of the World Cup series on television. Twenty-three minutes later, out at sea, 50 miles west of the thriving fishing town of Chimbote with its population of 200,000, the ocean bed cracked and heaved. The earth, tortured by stress, sought to find for itself a more comfortable position, like an old man turning in bed; and all along a 250-mile stretch of coastline, bounded by Trujillo in the north and Lima, the capital, in the south, the ground heaved and shook in a mighty earthquake which achieved an intensity of between seven and eight degrees on the Richter scale. For many hundreds of miles north, south and east across the land, the shock was felt.

At first the magnitude of the disaster was not appreciated. In Lima, people rushed into the streets, but the capital was fortunate and escaped without damage. Not for some hours, for all communications had been cut, was it learned that the full force of this 'act of God' had been felt by Chimbote, which lay on the narrow coastal plain, and by the towns and villages inland, in the foothills of the Andean mountain range.

Early reports, even then, seriously underestimated the magnitude of the disaster. They spoke of '250 killed in Chimbote' and '140 in Huaraz'. Slowly the shocking truth emerged: Chimbote lay in ruins and an estimated 2,700 people had died. Casma, Huanmey and all the towns along the coast had suffered to a greater or lesser extent, and unknown thousands of people had been killed. It was quite impossible to discover what had happened inland, in the district of Callejón de Huaylas, a popular tourist area known as the 'Switzerland of Peru', where lay hundreds of mountain towns and small villages.

Hurricanes batter Caribbean

At least 1,100 died and 150,000 were made homeless when Hurricane David lashed the Dominican Republic on 1 September 1979, with winds gusting to 150 mph. Nearly 12 months later, on 5 August 1980, another hurricane battered the Caribbean. Hurricane Allen caused nearly 100 deaths, mainly on the island of St Lucia.

Radio communication was silenced as a result of damage to the hydro-electric station at Huallanca; roads were impassable through landslides and subsidence; and when, next day, helicopters attempted to reconnoitre, the pilots' view was obscured by mist and huge clouds of dust rising thousands of feet into the air. Nobody knew what had happened in an area the size of Scotland, dominated by the 22,205-feet-high peak of Mount Huascaran.

An hour after the earthquake it was already apparent that the magnitude of the disaster was far greater than the authorities in Lima had originally imagined. The President of Peru, General Velasco, set sail in a naval vessel for Chimbote (for the coastal roads were blocked by landslides, the airfields were unusable and there was always the fear of further tremors) with various senior officials. The next morning he inspected the ruined town and neighbouring Casma and Coishco, and visited the injured at an emergency hospital. Before he returned to Lima – bringing some of the injured on the ship with him – in order to direct rescue operations, he attempted to visit the mountainous Callejón de Huaylas, but it was still impossible.

At Chimbote, General Velasco had found a town in ruins; 60–70 per cent of the buildings were destroyed, the old part of the town, where many buildings were in poor condition, being the worst affected. Almost nothing, whether concrete or adobe, had escaped damage. Despite the efforts of the rescue parties, dozens of people still lay under the rubble, injured and perhaps dying. Many hundreds more camped in the streets; some had no roof beneath which to shelter, others were afraid of further earth tremors.

From the Callejón de Huaylas, isolated behind rock-barred roads, confused and unconfirmed reports suggested even worse destruction. Aircraft were still hampered by bad visibility and vast dust-clouds. Eventually an amateur radio operator from within the mountain fastnesses managed to make contact and, with his plea 'Don't forget us!', the world first learned that the town of Yungay and a part of nearby Ranrahirca had completely disappeared under a landslide from Huascaran. Later, the Air Force confirmed this news: a vast wall of mud and snow had swept down the

Above: Survivors search for belongings.
Below: A campsite for the homeless

mountainside and, divided by a spur of hills, swallowed the two small towns.

Of Yungay, where the few survivors had managed to flee to the cemetery on the edge of the town, all that could be seen were the tips of the 100-feet-high palm trees which had stood in the main square. A helicopter pilot reported that he had counted a dozen more towns, each of between two and three thousand inhabitants, which were now merely heaps of stones.

For two and a half days no helicopter was able to land in the Andes region because of the continuing bad visibility. Until a hundred parachutists managed to land, the only contact with these isolated regions came from the desperate, pleading voice of the radio amateur.

The very size of the area of devastation meant that much of it was inaccessible, and it was many days before relief-workers – their resources stretched to the utmost – managed to reach remoter parts. One of the problems was to know just what supplies were needed. In the mountain villages hundreds of thousands of Indian peasants remained without heating, food or shelter for almost a week. Throughout the area survivors poured on to the passable roads on foot, in carts and lorries, desperately seeking help and refuge. Distracted people made for the nearest towns – often to find, like the two injured village policemen who staggered into Huaraz three days after the earthquake, that the hoped-for sources of assistance were themselves in desperate straits. Without the much-needed help the death-toll mounted steeply.

On the coastal plain rescue operations continued, and relief-workers and aid of all kinds poured in from all over the world. So great was the task in this region, scattered with huge *haciendas* farming sugar or maize, that in Chimbote, despite the all-pervading smell of fish-meal from the damaged factory, five days after the earthquake rescue workers could still use their noses to find more and more dead bodies under the rubble. And still the number of dead and dying in the mountain villages in a region some 300 miles long and 120 miles wide could only be guessed at.

The fear continued. From time to time small earth tremors could be felt and when, a couple of days after the earthquake, the ground again trembled,

---

Avalanche destroys sanatorium

Seventy one people, most of them under 15 years of age, were killed when an earth slide triggered by an avalanche of melting snow sent hundreds of tons of debris crashing into a tuberculosis sanatorium at Plateau d'Assy, near Mont Blanc in the French Alps, in mid-April, 1970.

people rushed into the streets in their night-clothes, their hands sheltering their heads. Many preferred to sleep in the open; and the new 'houses', built on the rubble of the old, were made of harmless rushes. Some feared even to sleep, for they had heard that the mountain lakes could break their natural barriers, causing disastrous floods.

This particular horror, however, was spared the luckless population. Although many valley streams turned into torrents, there was comparatively little damage from water; nor did a tidal-wave follow upon the earthquake, the ocean level varying only by a few feet from its normal level.

Rock falls and avalanches, however, had caused major damage. Of these, the greatest and most catastrophic was that which destroyed Yungay and Ranrahirca and killed nearly 30,000 people in these and in neighbouring small towns and villages. On that day, 5,000 feet up in the heights of Huascaran, a party of Japanese mountain climbers visiting this famous mountain resort found themselves the horrified but fascinated spectators of this event. The avalanche began with an almost vertical fall of 10,000 feet of a vast mass of ice and rock, almost a third of a mile wide and nearly two miles long, from the western face of Mount Huascaran. Impelled by the tremendous height of its initial fall, this gigantic mass then poured down the valley at a speed estimated at nearly 250 miles an hour. The million cubic yards of ice that had become detached from the highest point of the glacier then set another 24 million cubic yards in motion.

In the path of this unimaginable terror lay small villages and the towns of Yungay on the west and Ranrahirca on the east of a mountain spur. Above Yungay, a 600-foot hill was swept up in the path of the avalanche and deposited on the other side of the valley. This and the unfortunate mountain towns absorbed the force of the huge landslide. Other rock- and earth-falls blocked roads, particularly in the coastal areas where the road-side slopes were steep, dammed the River Santa at Recuhat, and destroyed countless houses. Many of these slides took place in stages, giving the threatened population time to flee: but in Yungay and Ranrahirca there was small hope of escaping the roaring death . . . and only eight years after Ranrahirca and seven mountain villages had been the previous victims of the Nevado de Huascaran's monstrous ice-cap, when a part of it broke loose killing 3,000 people.

It took many weeks for the people of the devastated regions to recover from the effects of 'the giant's hand', as one Indian peasant called it, and the villages in the steep Andean valleys, tucked under the towering cliffs, suffered most severely through their sheer inaccessibility. Freezing rain made it even more difficult for troops and parachutists to reach the population.

Guns set off avalanche

Austrian troops stationed in the Alps during World War I began firing their cannon in practice one December morning in 1916. The reverberations set off an avalanche in which more than 2,000 people are believed to have died.

In the valleys life came back to normal more quickly. The 'uncomprehending silence', which one observer reported as brooding over shattered towns, turned to the noise and bustle of people trying to rebuild shattered lives. And when, on 2 June, Peru beat Bulgaria in a World Cup match, people even found the heart to cheer, and red-and-white Peruvian flags were planted to wave proudly over pathetic heaps of rubble that had once been homes.

Thousands of people without homes tried to organize new lives – and many realized they would be homeless for a long time. For many, too, there were no more jobs. Young people with knapsacks took to the roads, making for the sugar capital in the north, Trujillo. 'What is the point', one asked 'of rebuilding here?' And indeed with the trade of the towns disrupted and with little, poorly paid, work available on the *haciendas*, their reactions were reasonable. Once again it was the mountain peasants, who knew no other way of life, who suffered most harshly.

It seemed that the whole of Peru and half the world were anxious to help in the vast task of rehabilitation. Peruvian authorities encouraged visits from journalists and notable foreigners who would tell the rest of the world what had happened, and thus recruit much needed aid of all kinds.

Where any disaster is concerned the question that is always asked afterwards is: 'What could have been done to prevent it?' Where natural events are concerned, particularly in the case of one so overwhelming as the Peruvian earthquake, the answer must be 'Very little'. Most of man's protection must lie in warnings which are the result of constant vigilance. Hurricane, flood and avalanche warnings are now commonplace in many parts of the world; and even if they are sometimes too late, they help to save many lives. Predicting an earthquake is more difficult, but the steady series of major disasters to which the world is prone makes it apparent that research into both the prevention and warning of earthquakes is of vital importance.

The imminence of an earthquake can sometimes be detected by continuous monitoring of the fluctuations of the earth's magnetic field, its seismic activities and the strain and tilt of the earth's crust. Just as a threatened ice-fall can be safely triggered off, under controlled conditions, by the use of explosives, so explosives and drilling techniques could be used to provoke land movement and unlock dangerous faults under strain. So far, however, this is a science which has made few practical advances and 'the giant's hand' continues to crush and maim throughout the world.

Many lessons were learned from Peru's disaster. It became apparent that destruction would have been less if buildings had been better sited or better constructed. In the area affected by the worst of the earthquake, the damage was caused mainly to buildings which were of poor quality, unsuited to the type of soil on which they were constructed, and erected on badly laid foundations. The earthquake opened cracks in the saturated sand and clay soils and increased the level of underground water; while rock-sited foundations were not so seriously affected. In Huaraz, for example, the older parts of the town, built on the alluvium of the river, suffered the greatest damage; the new part, however, built on rock brought down by a landslide in 1941, was less damaged. Mud-brick buildings proved to be less equal to strain than brick or concrete, but in some cases concrete buildings collapsed because of the poor materials used in their construction.

These lessons are learnt at a fearful cost. In the final analysis, man's puny efforts are all useless when Nature decides to unleash the full fury of her powers.

Mass Poisoning in Iraq (1971–1972)

Desperate measures to overcome a famine disaster led to an even greater catastrophe in the Middle Eastern state of Iraq in the winter of 1971–72. For, although the government took what it thought were the correct measures to provide grain for its ten million people after two years of severe drought, it failed to take account of human failings like greed and impatience. The result was what is believed to be the greatest mass poisoning in history, which left more than 5,000 victims dead and tens of thousands more maimed for life.

In Old Testament times, and even before that, the people of what we now call Iraq were among the most civilized on earth. The city of Babylon stands on the edge of the area between the rivers Euphrates and Tigris christened Mesopotamia by the Greeks. But time has stood still here over the centuries while other nations and cultures have developed new lifestyles and more prosperous ways of earning a living. It remains a largely agricultural area of small towns and villages, its people ekeing a meagre existence from their arid, sun-scorched fields. The summers of 1969 and 1970 were even drier than usual. Grain crops were abysmal, and stockpiles had to be raided to provide enough for the nation to eat. By 1971, what remained in granary warehouses was at a perilously low level.

The ruling Ba'ath Party decided to buy foreign seed to make up the deficiencies. The best available was Mexipak, a high-yield wheat strain developed in Mexico by American Nobel Prize winner Dr Norman Borlaug. The Iraqis ordered 73,000 tons of it, mainly from an American company, and topped it up with a separate order for 22,000 tons of barley from U.S. west coast suppliers. But Iraq insisted that all the grain be chemically treated against plant disease. The most effective means of doing this was by methylmercury dicyandiamide.

America, Canada and most of Europe banned the use of mercury-based treatments after poison scares in Sweden, Pakistan and Guatamala in the 1950s, for though the silver-coloured liquid metal is useful in fighting disease, it is also lethal to humans and animals, particularly when swallowed. Iraq itself had suffered mercury-poisoning epidemics in both 1956 and 1960. But in a land where the grain yield was so vital, the authorities could not afford to wait until an equally reliable seed treatment was discovered.

On 16 September 1971, the freighter *Trade Carrier*, registered in Liberia, arrived at the southern Iraq port of Basra with the precious stocks of wheat and barley. The grain was a vivid pink colour after the mercury treatment, and each sack carried a poison warning. The wheat, mainly from Mexico, carried the Spanish words 'No usarla para alimento' while the barley had the same warning in English: 'Do not use for food'. There were also skull-and-crossbones logos, with the prominent words 'Poison Treated'.

Sadly, few Iraqis speak Spanish or English. And that ignorance was soon to prove fatal. So was the method adopted by the authorities to distribute the sorely-needed grain. Farmers were told they would not have to pay for it until it was harvested, in a year's time. Consequently, many decided to enjoy a prosperous year on credit by selling all the wheat they had been able to grow, despite the droughts, and filling their empty bins with the 'free' seed. Too many forgot to keep some grain back to make their own bread for the winter.

Lorry drivers were under strict instructions to drive straight from the docks to distribution warehouses. Yet some still arrived with part of their loads missing, claiming they had been robbed along the road. And some warehouses ignored the order to get a signed statement from customers, to the effect that they realised the new wheat and barley had been mercury-treated. As an additional warning, the Iraqi government had a plane drop half-a-million leaflets over agricultural areas. It was hardly a fool-proof method of alerting an increasingly hungry populace to the perils they faced if they used the seed for anything other than planting.

Soon wives and mothers all over Iraq were overcoming the qualms of their husbands and baking the grain into bread. Many of the survivors later told hospital authorities it was the best bread they had ever tasted. Families began stockpiling the seed for baking when special guests were expected. But within weeks the awful consequences of those tasty meals were seen everywhere. Children and adults were vomiting violently. Those who did not collapse found it impossible to keep their balance or co-ordinate their actions. Mercury attacks the brain and the nervous system.

The grain sacks contained information on what to do if treated seed was swallowed. They said: 'Give milk or white of eggs beaten with water, then a tablespoon of salt in a glass of warm water, and repeat until vomit fluid is clear. Repeat milk or white of eggs with water. Call a physician.' But they said it in English. And many of the victims were in no physical condition to call anybody. They lay helpless on their beds or where they fell, and were lucky if neighbours arrived in time to whisk them to hospital.

By Christmas, all the big city hospitals were crammed with poisoned peasants, and by January medical centres in all 14 Iraqi provinces were reporting hundreds of new arrivals every day. The government issued urgent warnings, ordering that all the contaminated seed be immediately returned to distribution warehouses. On no account should it be fed to humans or animals. The penalty for disobedience was death.

A month later the crisis took on another dimension. Poisoned beef was found in butchers' shops. Farmers who had fed their beasts the pink barley were now trying to get rid of their ailing animals before they lost too much weight. The government closed all abattoirs, and prescribed the eating of fresh or frozen meat for two months. Many Iraqis maintained a voluntary ban for much longer, and prices of alternative foods spiralled.

Official government figures put the total poisoned at 6,530, and listed 459 hospital deaths. But outside experts put the toll much higher. Edward Hughes, a Middle East writer for both the *Wall Street Journal* and *Time Magazine*, who wrote about the poison outbreak for the British *Sunday Times* in 1973, said: 'My investigations and private estimates of doctors and government officials on the scene suggest that as many as 6,000 died, and perhaps 100,000 were injured. Many of the ill never left their home villages; many of the dead were buried in unmarked graves.'

Hughes also wrote graphically of what he saw when he visited Iraq nearly two years after the poison grain disaster. 'I found hundreds of square miles of human devastation' he said. 'Hardly a village in the broad plain between the Tigris and Euphrates is without its victims. Entire families have been wiped out. I even saw one abandoned settlement where everyone had died or fled. I could not get its name, for there was no-one to ask, except a bent old crone on a nearby dirt trail; she uttered only a shrill "Doctor, doctor", pointing her stick feebly towards a larger town in the distance.'

Perhaps, though, the dead were the lucky ones. Hughes continued: 'As my car came to a crossroads, the driver gasped and braked. A dozen maimed youngsters aged 6 to 12 were trying to play football. Several of them lurched and reeled grotesquely, as if drunk, while others stood with vacant stares.

The Bermuda Triangle

A flight of five Grumman US Navy bombers took off from Fort Lauderdale, Florida, for a training flight on 5 December 1945. Two hours later, all contact with them was lost. A Martin bomber was dispatched to search for the missing planes. Twenty minutes later, it too disappeared. No trace of any of the planes or their crews of 27 men was ever found. The area in which they vanished later became famous as the 'Bermuda Triangle'.

'One lad of ten staggered uncertainly towards the ball, but as he kicked, his balance failed and he tumbled to the ground, writhing in frustration. Suddenly a small squealing boy ran across the courtyard, arms outstretched, to retrieve the ball for himself. Only when the boy fell headlong into a large bush did we realise with horror that he was almost totally blind.'

Science was the only winner from the disaster. After the last of the victims had stumbled home, the doctors unable to do anything more for the afflictions of feeling, sight, hearing and balance that would stay with the patients for life, the Baghdad authorites invited a team from Rochester University, New York State, to study the tragic effects of the catastrophe. The experts, led by Dr Thomas Clarkson, discovered, among other things, that mothers can pass mercury on to their unborn babies – one child was found to have three times the mercury concentration of the mother in his blood – and that certain resins can speed up the process of the body rejecting mercury.

But a failsafe antidote for mercury poisoning has yet to be found. And until seed sellers come up with an equally infallible fungicide treatment, until they label poisons in a language the users of their product can understand, and until human nature does not unwisely take advantage of situations it does not fully comprehend, the risk of an equally horrific outbreak of death and devastation in underdeveloped countries will always be with us.

Isle of Man Summerland Fire (1973)

Summerland was a dream come true for holidaymakers. It was 'Britain's first forget-the-weather family fun centre', according to the people who ran it. And Trust House Forte Leisure Ltd also proudly boasted that it was the largest indoor holiday resort in the world. On six brightly-lit floors beneath a pyramid-shaped solarium dome, trippers could while away grey days on slot machines in amusement arcades, play bingo, enjoy sauna baths, or relax in six bars and a restaurant. They could lounge on deck chairs amid potted palms, watching a live show, while their children enjoyed their own fun fair or the roller-skate disco in the basement.

The councillors of the island's capital, Douglas, were delighted with their £2 million investment. Some had been uneasy about waiving a local by-law to approve the building, but in the two years since it opened it had certainly helped amuse the tourists who were the lifeblood of many of the island's 56,000 residents. More than half a million had sampled its delights in the summer of 1972.

But on the evening of 2 August 1973, just 25 months after Summerland opened for business, the lucrative dream became a nightmare – and cost 50 people, ten of them children, their lives in a horrifying inferno.

Chilling drizzle had driven nearly 3,000 holidaymakers into the warmth of the fun centre, grafted into the cliff face at the northern end of the front. The 96 feet high building could hold more, but latecomers found most of the bars on the lower floors packed. In the vast Marquee Show bar, a three-man band was entertaining crowds beneath the transparent dome, above which the sky was darkening towards dusk.

Elsewhere, bingo players scanned their cards to the sound of laughter and chat from happy drinkers. In the basement, disc jockey Johnny Silver introduced a beat group who played the latest hits for energetic dancers. Then the voice of schoolteacher William Hefin Roberts, from Winsford, Cheshire, cut across the babble. It said: 'There's a fire out there.'

At first, Mr Roberts recalled, the man on duty at the main door seemed to take no notice. Then he spoke into a walkie-talkie radio. Mr Roberts ran towards the end wall of the complex to see if he could help fight the fire. The audience in the Marquee Show Bar also noticed the smoke. Eric Taylor, 51-year-old organist with the group entertaining the crowds, quipped: 'There appears to be a little fire – let's put it out with The Blue Danube.' But though the music went on, the people listening became uneasy. Some left their seats, only to return sheepishly when a Summerland employee joked about a chip-pan fire.

Ken Harding, the fun centre's technical services manager, was by this time leading the fire-fighters. Two staff were outside, trying to extinguish flames in a disused kiosk reached from the promenade by a concrete spiral staircase. The kiosk was attached to the wall of Summerland, and Harding, playing a hose on it from inside the building, urged his colleagues to pull the kiosk away with flagpoles. But it was already too late.

'The flames were shooting 20 to 30 feet high and licking the steel cladding of the main building,' Harding said later. 'I could see the steel was warping and opening with the heat, so I ran back and gave the alarm.'

On the upper floors, customers had already decided the billowing smoke was reason enough to leave. But as they made their way down the staircases, that smoke thickened. The kiosk fire had spread underneath the restaurant floor, bursting out again in an amusement arcade at the centre of the building. Acrid black fumes shot through with flames whirled up towards the acrylic dome of the building, forcing those descending to try to turn round in the crush. Suddenly, clothes and hair caught alight. Children and babies were dropped over the stair-rail to willing hands below. Other parents tried to battle against the tide of people, searching desperately for their families.

'The fire seemed to spread in seconds, it was terrible,' said one survivor. 'Mothers were screaming, tearing round looking for their children. It was absolute confusion.' Another said: 'There were children crying for their mummies and daddies, and there were daddies and mummies crying in anguish for their little ones with no idea where they were. It was more than the mind could bear.' A woman who ran a shop in the complex said: 'Everybody was dashing for the exits. I was knocked down in the rush. I was flat on my stomach and people were trampling over me. There was a kiddy under me. I managed to get her to safety.'

Wyn Price, manageress of the sauna baths on the top floor, said: 'Black smoke filled the building and then the flames came rushing up towards us. I dashed into the sauna and told everybody to get out. Then suddenly a sheet of flame shot across our floor level. I managed to get out through an emergency exit down some side stairs. I don't know if the people in the sauna got out. They were all in their underclothes.'

In the basement, children fled the dance floor. Two 14-year-olds, Sharon Walter and Sharon Smith, later told reporters: 'We tried to get out through a back door but we could not get it open. Burning plastic was dripping from the ceiling and someone put covers over us to keep it off us. Eventually we got out through a side door. We saw one person break a window to escape, and a man still wearing roller skates jump through another window.' Sharon Smith's parents were waiting in uncertainty outside. 'My wife flaked out two or three times,' Mr Smith recalled. 'I thought I was never going to see the girls alive again.'

Disc jockey Silver ushered 200 youngsters to safety, then went back into the fumes to try to save more people. He seriously injured his leg breaking the fall of a child thrown down from a higher floor. He was not the only hero. Entertainments manager Ted Oldham smashed a big window and handed children to willing helpers outside. And 6ft 5in Irish staff member Noel Quigley plucked youngsters off the floor and hurled them to safety through the front doors. 'He must have saved 50 or 60 like that,' a colleague said later. 'They were being trampled underfoot around him and even at his size he was knocked over several times.'

The understandable panic of those fleeing the flames was heightened when they found several escape routes locked. Staff smashed through doors into the adjacent Aquadrome swimming pool to lead some of those trapped to safety. And glass in two secured doors at the main entrance was smashed by holidaymakers. Alan Sandham, 17, from Salford, Lancashire, said: 'I tried three emergency doors that were chained or locked. I was told later it was to keep gate-crashers out. Lots of people panicked when they found doors chained. I saw people standing there tearing at the doors instead of running to find others that weren't locked. I can't help thinking the time that was wasted may have cost them their lives.'

Belfast holidaymaker Sam Farr said: 'A lot of people had to kick their way out through glass panels in the side of the building. Glass was melting in the heat. I saw one man with his hair on fire and his coat melted off his back, running with a youngster in his arms.' Mrs Elizabeth Arthurs, also from Belfast, who was drinking with her husband while their five children enjoyed the basement play area, said: 'We ran out of the Marquee Bar just before the floors collapsed in on other people. Some children with roller skates on were unable to run out.'

Her husband Peter said: 'About 100 people were lying on the ground where they had fallen, shouting and screaming. It was pandemonium. Emergency doors were locked and people started smashing glass. People were crawling over others lying near the doors. You could hear limbs cracking.'

Lorry driver Robert Bore, 46, from Skelmersdale, Lancashire, was on his way into Summerland with his wife when the fire began. He said: 'An inferno seemed to engulf the whole building. I removed one lady with face

The Summerland holiday centre in flames

injuries from the main entrance. I had just gone back for a second woman who had terrible leg burns when an explosion nearly blew us off our feet. I was within a few feet of the main entrance but it was impossible to get in to rescue anyone because of a solid sheet of flame. No-one could have got out through there.'

Those who reached fresh air stood sobbing on the promenade, staring at each stunned, shocked and scorched survivor who lurched out of the smoke. Was it a relative, a friend? The worst hurt were rushed to Douglas's Noble Hospital, in ambulances or holidaymakers' cars, volunteered or commandeered by police. As the walking wounded comforted each other, grisly visions of the less lucky ones appeared behind them, silhouettes against the raging flames, leaping screaming to the ground or motionless in the steel skeleton of the gutted building.

Holidaymakers and residents rushed to help the rescue services with first aid, paperwork and administration. The manager of the nearby Palace Hotel and Casino said: 'Almost everyone in the hotel left meals on tables to go and see what they could do. So did taxi drivers, hotel people, coach hire firms and people with private cars. We appealed through the hotel for volunteer blood donors and 20 people – all in their holiday clothes – came forward straight away. Food and holidays were forgotten. Everybody just wanted to help.'

The fire, fought by 93 of the island's 106 firemen on their total complement of 16 engines, was under control in just over an hour. In the blackened building, 12 bodies lay in a dark, narrow, windowless emergency staircase, all asphyxiated by the lethal fumes. On another narrow flight, 13 more tourists had been burned or trampled to death. But, almost miraculously, another survivor was discovered in the ruins. Barman Graham Harding, 19, had crawled under a storeroom sink and covered himself with a water-soaked jacket. He was unconscious but still alive.

Seven of his colleagues were not so lucky. Summerland held a staff roll call at 11 a.m. next day. It confirmed the worst fears of one girl among the 250 on the payroll. 'I have been up all night looking for two boys from our digs,' she said. 'Now they are not here.'

Identifying the horribly-burned corpses laid out in St George's church hall was an ordeal for relatives and a headache for the authorities. A policeman said: 'God help those who come to identify them – its worse than a bloody war.'

Frederick Allen, 60, and his wife Frances, 54, were also among the dead. They had come to Douglas to celebrate their silver wedding anniversary.

Mourning blanketed northern England and Ulster – it was peak season for Irish holidays on the Isle of Man. Manx people were devastated. The island

Girls die in factory

More than 145 workers, most of them teenage girls, died when a blaze in a fabric wastebin quickly spread through the premises of the Triangle Shirtwaist Company in New York's Manhattan on Saturday, 25 March 1911. The cramped factory was on the eighth and ninth floor of the ten-storey Asch building, on the corner of Washington Place and Greene Street. Only 12 girls reached the lift before acrid fumes made waiting for its return impossible. Ladders reached only the sixth floor, and firemen's hoses could reach only the seventh. Onlookers watched helplessly as terrified girls broke windows and leapt 85 feet to their deaths and the weight of other bodies brought down the flimsy fire escape stairs. The press of panic-stricken workers made it impossible to use inward-opening doors. In 18 minutes, the victims were all dead. More than 100,000 angry mourners attended a mass funeral.

had never suffered such a disaster. But the sorrow quickly turned to fury and frustration. How could such a catastrophe strike a supposedly-fireproof construction, the biggest new building on the island for a century?

It quickly became clear that Oroglas, a Perspex-like acrylic used in much of the construction, was partly responsible for the fire spreading so quickly and lethally. Summerland was the first big building to use it extensively, and construction chiefs in Britain were quick to point out that it would never have been allowed on the mainland, where strict building regulations limited the use of plastics and insisted on better means of escape.

London fire prevention officer Ronald Miller said: 'Plastic always causes problems. There is always very dense, toxic smoke and plastic melts and, still alight, drops all over the place, spreading fire more rapidly than ever. If I had been shown a description of this centre before it was built, I would have warned the planners they were creating a potential fire hazard.'

Lessons clearly had to be learned from the experience everyone had gained the tragic way. Manx Lieutenant-Governor Sir Peter Stallard appointed three outsiders – a judge, a Home Office inspector of fire services and a building professor, all from England – as a commission of inquiry. After hearing 91 witnesses over 49 days, they reported that the catastrophe was due to an amazing accumulation of human error and failure, but there were 'no villains'.

The commission said the fire was started, either accidentally or maliciously, by three boys playing in the ruined glass kiosk. The Galbestos coating caught fire six minutes later, and flames built up unnoticed in the concealed gap for 15 minutes before bursting through the Decalin the amusement arcade. Thirty tons of softwood flooring and wooden joists, plus the flame-hungry Oroglas of the roof and walls, turned the blaze into a holocaust. A sprinkler system, which would have cost £250,000, might have helped stem the flames, but the local authority had not insisted on one.

The commission's ruling that there had been 'no villains' stunned Manx islanders, who feared the catastrophe could ruin their tourist trade. 'If this is not villainy, what is?' screamed one local newspaper. Another reporter lamented that, as a layman, he had accepted the word of experts when he had a premonition of fire disaster while inspecting Summerland as it was built. Sadly, too many people who should have known better had done the same thing, and a seemingly-unrelated series of errors and omissions, each of which was not in itself fatal, had snowballed into a disaster. Fifty lives had been sacrificed to the lesson that well-intentioned progress should not be at the expense of the accepted wisdom of rules based on experience and common sense.

Ermenonville Forest Air Crash (1974)

Flags of 18 nations, topped with black crepe, fluttered over the scene. A thousand people, many still suffering the shock of their bereavement two months earlier, stood in silence. They were only a tiny fraction of those who had wanted to be there, at Thiais, near Orly airport. The others could only mourn in their native lands, hundreds, thousands, of miles away.

Few could understand more than a small part of the ceremony. It was opened in English by the Vicar of the Anglican Church in Paris. After him came Catholics, Jews, priests of the Armenian Christian Church, mullahs from Turkey, Morocco and Pakistan, Buddhist priests from Japan, and a holy man from India.

Perhaps the words of M. Achille-Fould, French Aviation Minister, were the most moving: 'The world-wide family of all in aviation is in mourning. May the earth of France lie easily on those we commit to it. France, too, looks on them as her own children.' It was France's epitaph on history's greatest air disaster.

Though a few bodies had been identified and handed over to relatives for burial, most of the staggering, tragic, total of 346 instantly killed men, women and children were being committed to a foreign grave on this spring Thursday of 9 May, 1974. The actual burial would not be public; that would take place in a few days' time, using heavy earth-moving machinery.

The worst air disaster in history had taken almost twice as many lives as any single accident before. At the time of writing, it still holds that unenviable record. It was what every airline had dreaded: an accident to a fully loaded, wide-body jet. As the mystery unfolded, grief gave way to bitterness. It *need* not have happened; it *should* not have happened. Who was to blame?

The DC10 of Turkish Airlines had flown in from Turkey and made a perfect landing at Orly Airport near Paris. Weather conditions were good on that early spring Sunday morning, 3 March, and the pilot taxied briskly up to the terminal buildings; almost immediately passengers started to embark and fill up his lightly-loaded aircraft, while those who had just landed were asked to stay on board. According to airline officials, 216 adult passengers and one infant embarked at Orly.

The need to get more than 200 people on a flight for which they had not booked meant that documentation was hasty. It seemed over the next harrowing hours that not all of the passengers had been listed; at least one man was travelling on a passport not his own, and some were using other people's tickets.

The plane re-started its three giant General Electric jets, and taxied along to the take-off runway at a few minutes past noon, carrying 335 passengers and 11 crew. In two minutes the DC10 was off, climbing powerfully into the bright sunny sky of France, the three engines – one under each wing, a third in the tail – belching vapour and exhaust. The time: 12.30 p.m.

The plane climbed fast on a wide eastern sweep to skirt Paris. Flight plans ordained that when eventually it turned to its north-west course for London it would be at 16,000 feet. Controllers of France's Northern Air Region watched it on their radar screens as it reached a height of 13,000 feet.

And then, quite simply, the plane vanished from all screens.

At 12.35 it crashed into a shallow depression within the Ermenonville State Forest north-east of Paris.

On that warm Sunday there were many people strolling along the numerous wooded pathways, but although the huge aircraft ploughed a thousand-yard furrow through the trees, shearing them off before kinetic energy was expended and the wreckage had come to rest, no-one on the ground was hurt.

It happened without any warning. Some claimed to have seen the aircraft explode in the sky; others had seen it under apparently perfect control, seeming to make an approach towards some not-too-distant airfield. Others, more expert, had seen it in difficulties at a low altitude, trying to drag its nose up from a shallow dive.

Thirty-five minutes after the crash, rescuers arrived by helicopter. One glance showed their journey had been in vain. Little fires, like those of an Indian village, were separated by hundreds of yards, indicating where parts of the engines and fuel system had ended. Bits of fuselage and the débris of human possessions were strewn over the ground; tatters of clothing festooned the branches of trees which had escaped destruction. No one could have survived for an instant.

Meanwhile, at London's Heathrow Airport, there was alarm as the DC10 became first late, then overdue. Anxious relatives awaiting the return of more than two hundred British passengers, demanded news. When it came, an elderly man collapsed, a young woman attacked the press with a stiletto-heel shoe and a man smashed press cameras. Mingled with the horror were elements of desperate hope, total incomprehension. Which of the London-bound passengers had transferred to the Turkish airliner? How could a plane, so fast, so safe and foolproof, just plunge to earth on a clear spring

Firemen carry away the remains of the DC10 passengers

The landing gear wheel amongst the strewn wreckage

day? But it had.

The 'black box', which had automatically recorded all the aircraft's movements, was recovered intact, but it merely stated that the plane had reached 13,000 feet and then dived to a lower altitude before crashing – a fact already well-established. Ground controllers reported having heard a few seconds of excited, unintelligible speech before total silence when the DC10 left their radar screens. This suggested a disaster at 13,000 feet, and not an incomprehensible exercise in hedge-hopping.

The most popular theory was a bomb, but aircraft authorities were adamant that all passengers and luggage had been screened.

A fortnight later: the probable truth. Bodies had been found, still strapped in their seats, a full seven miles from the rest of the wreckage. Then the aircraft's rear cargo door was found, nine miles away, and this seemed to be the missing clue.

Two years before, in Canada, the faulty latch on a DC10 cargo door had nearly caused a similar trajedy. The door had opened suddenly in flight and this, for a reason which was not at first clear to the highly skilled crew, seemed to jam a number of the controls. Somehow they nursed it back to base.

The United States Federal Aviation Administration gave instructions for doors to be modified so that it was impossible for them to open in flight. Further recommendations were made to the manufacturer, McDonnell-Douglas of California, that the floor of the passenger compartment, immediately above the hold, should be strengthened and air vents made in it. This expensive modification would have to be for subsequent aircraft: meanwhile, the doors must be corrected; and McDonnell-Douglas passed on these comparatively simple instructions to all its customers.

Comparison with the near-disaster over Canada proved that the Turkish plane's cargo door had opened at 13,000 feet. This, as over Canada, had caused instant depressurization of the lower, cargo compartment. As in every section of a modern airliner, the cargo compartment was kept at an air pressure approximating to that on the ground; and when this pressure dropped suddenly the light passenger deck immediately above it collapsed. In the more serious Turkish case it dragged seats down into the hold, sucking a number of them in which occupants were still strapped out of the open doorway.

At this point the pilot might have been able to dive safely to a lower altitude – but the control cables of a DC10, from flight deck to tail, run under the passenger deck, and in the Turkish aircraft these were instantly and completely jammed. Helpless, the aircraft fell into a shallow dive which no pilot could have righted.

The recovered door showed that a vital flange, part of the safety modification, was missing. There was no doubt that it had been fitted but no certainty as to when it had come adrift. A cargo handler at Orly was for a time under suspicion of not having closed the door before take-off and

Football stars killed

Eight star soccer players, including four top England internationals, were among 23 people killed when a British European Airways airliner crashed trying to take off from icy Munich airport, West Germany, on 6 February 1958. The players, all from Manchester United, were returning from a successful European Cup match in Belgrade, Yugoslavia.

furthermore of having been unable to read the instructions printed on it, but he and the airport authorities were able to dispel this suspicion.

Exactly a year later, a group of English people were taken to the scene by a French friend. The whole area had been enclosed by a high fence, and they had to be let in by the *Garde Forestière*. They looked around them in horror at the wreckage, the minutiae of human tragedy, the bits of clothing, luggage and the rest. It would take years to retrieve all this, and the French government had decided the job should not be done by souvenir hunters, hence the enclosure.

'Yes', said the *Garde Forestière*, 'he might have made it, you know, that pilot from Turkey, he might have saved many lives because the place where he came down was fairly clear. But, *hélas*, he hit this rocky eminence here. And the plane simply broke up, wings, everything, going everywhere. That is why the felled bit of Ermonenville Forest is so large, why the fence has to be so long . . .'

Almost two years after the tragedy the first of many claims from dependents and relatives of those who died was settled in an American court. Others, of course, would follow. The sum awarded was large; as much punitive, some said, as compensatory – in order, perhaps, to impress upon all concerned that something of this sort should never, could never, happen again.

American Mid-West Tornadoes (1974)

For the people of the Gulf and Mid-western states of the U.S.A. the word 'Twister' holds terror. Even the sound of an approaching tornado is awesome; anyone unlucky enough to be in the direct path of a tornado without any shelter available has little chance of surviving it.

In April 1974, in the worst tornado disaster since 1925 (when nearly 700 people were killed), a total of 324 people became victims of tornadoes in the space of eight hours, and hundreds more were injured, while damage ran into many millions of dollars. Although warnings had been given, a part of the area which was struck in 1974 was unfamiliar with tornadoes, and this contributed to the high death-toll.

Nothing can be done to prevent tornadoes and little is known about them, although no storm is more violent. Unlike hurricanes, which can be observed from within, tornadoes are so small that their study has not been practical. The conditions which give rise to them, however, are well-known and are present when warm moist air-masses meet cold dry air-masses.

Precipitating the events of 2 and 3 April 1974 was the swift eastward movement of an egg-shaped mass of cool dry air about one thousand miles across, while at the centre of the air-mass was a region of low pressure similar to that found in the calm eye of a hurricane.

This low pressure region moved very fast from central Kansas to Iowa and then on to the northern tip of Michigan. In the northern hemisphere air circulates counter-clockwise, round a centre of high or low pressure. Winds to the east of the cool air-mass were moving north, and by 2 April this northward flow was carrying moist air from the Gulf of Mexico which was rapidly warming up with the coming of spring and evaporating large masses of water.

Meanwhile about 200 miles to the landward, westward edge of the air-mass a cold front, flowing off the Rocky Mountains, developed, and a series of squall-lanes (instability lines) were formed. There the moist air welled upwards rapidly, spurring a compensating downward flow of cooler air from above and the series of squall-lines brought tornadoes over Alabama, like 'jabs from a boxer' as a meteorologist described it.

Research shows that tornadoes arise within small cyclones, a few miles across, which in turn arise within large thunderstorms. In the funnel of a tornado winds may swirl at 300 miles an hour or more – four times as fast as those in a hurricane. The movement of a tornado has been likened to a dancer, pirouetting on a rotating platform which is itself mounted on a truck, and this accounts for the terrifyingly erratic and unpredictable route many tornadoes take. At the edge of the tornado-funnel trees are uprooted; in the centre, buildings explode and railway carriages are blown over. The twister may be only 100 feet across, but it can leave a trail of damage half a mile wide.

On those two days in April 100 twisters struck in the space of eight hours in an area from Alabama to Windsor, Ontario, across the Canadian border. Two of the worst hit towns were Xenia, Ohio, and Brandenburg, Kentucky, and neither town had much experience of the killing twisters; there had been only seven tornadoes in the Xenia area in the last 24 years, and no deaths, and Brandenburg had never experienced a tornado before.

Since tornadoes strike more than a thousand times a year in the United States, people living in the affected regions have learnt to take shelter when warnings are given; to leave their cars if they cannot drive clear of the twister's path and find some hollow, if they can, in which to hide; to keep away from windows which can shatter; to take cover under large pieces of furniture. In the worst areas the houses are built with storm cellars in which the occupants can take refuge.

In the late afternoon, against a sky filled with blackness and flying débris, one particular twister roared its way through Xenia from the south-west, slashing a path of destruction three or four miles long and several hundred yards wide. New housing developments, old neighbourhoods, schools, churches, downtown businesses and a shopping centre, suffered equally. Within five minutes of sudden, shattering destruction 30 people died, nearly a hundred were injured, and thousands made homeless.

The people who had managed to take shelter emerged dazed, once the roaring inferno had passed, and took stock. They knew that the windows had shattered, for flying glass had rained upon them as they lay on the floors of the downstairs rooms, but out in the streets they discovered that almost every house had lost its roof and many their first floors. Some were virtually heaps of rubble and splinters. Dangling wires, loose signs, branches, traffic-lights – all were strewn higgledy-piggledy across once orderly streets.

Cars had been tossed along the roads; a train passing through the town with a load of new cars was safe, but all the cars were dented and their glass broken. Débris littered the streets blown from miles away and among it, untouched by the wind – such is the caprice of tornadoes – stood bizarre objects: a child's scooter, dressing-table ornaments, a pile of magazines, just as they had been left before the twister had reduced everything to chaos.

The town of Monticello lies in ruins

Tornado hits Chicago

Hailstones 'as big as pigeon's eggs' rained on Chicago on 28 March 1920, giving warning of the onslaught of a terrifying tornado. Cars were hurled through the air and houses shattered. One home was lifted up and turned upside down. Twenty eight people died and damage totalled $3 million.

At least half of Xenia had been destroyed and all the services disrupted. But by the next day the immense task of clearing up had already begun. Electricity was partly restored, and hundreds of volunteers came to help the population search for what remained of their possessions and to find some kind of shelter. A state of emergency was declared and national guardsmen – much of whose time was later spent in keeping sightseers away – were ordered out in Xenia, in Louisville, Kentucky, and in similarly stricken towns throughout the states of Alabama, Ohio, Indiana and Tennessee. In these states people sifted through the splinters that had been their homes, scraped the débris from the streets and sawed up fallen trees. There was a strange calm as with 'serene faces and certain hands' – as one reporter described it – the volunteers cleared up the rubbish against a background of persistent siren wails.

Throughout the affected areas stories abounded of individual incidents such as that at Windsor, where the roof was ripped off the local curling rink, killing and injuring those in its path, while the bodies of those who had been inside were found scattered over the neighbouring fields; and the metal frame warehouse of a construction company in Fountaintown, Indiana, which was lifted off the ground and carried a mile.

Perhaps one of the saddest results of the tornado's vicious attack was the effect it had upon the 1,600 people living in Brandenburg, Kentucky, 32 miles west of Louisville. This small farming community sat on the banks of the Ohio River, and most of its inhabitants had lived there all their lives. It was a small society, intimate, chatty and with an air of permanence. Its local paper was small and gossipy, and everybody knew everybody and all about each other. Modest houses, mostly of nineteenth-century architecture, stood on top of a pair of hills; the pace of life of Brandenburg was slow and restrained – it was 'a Mark Twain town'.

A few minutes of unleashed fury changed all this. Twenty-nine people died and scores were injured. Hundreds of people were made homeless as three-quarters of the buildings were damaged beyond repair. One 21-year-old girl and her 9-year-old brother were in a flat in an old two-storey house, clutching each other in terror as the tornado swept eastwards along the river's edge. Thirty seconds later they were trapped by wreckage while the neighbours in the flat downstairs – a woman and three young children – lay dead. The neighbour's infant daughter was found, in a field at the bottom of a hill 200 yards away, alive.

Later the river was dragged for bodies, as eye-witnesses spoke of houses, cars and bodies flying through the air. Such was the extent and importance of the destruction in this small community that many people decided to leave. It seemed pointless, they said, to try to rebuild: too much had gone for ever; the river town of Brandenburg had all but disappeared.

Months passed before the damage caused throughout the country could be repaired – it was estimated that damage to personal property alone had cost the country £1,000,000,000, and low-interest personal loans to home-owners and businessmen were immediately announced. Damage to property can be made good, but nothing can replace a way of life.

The Honduras Hurricane (1974)

Until September 1974 Honduras was to most people only the name of a country, somewhere in Central America. An unparalleled disaster was to change all that, for by press, radio and television, the almost unknown became suddenly and dramatically familiar.

Honduras lies on the Caribbean in the north and the Pacific in the south and south-west, with Nicaragua to the east, Guatemala to the west and El Salvador to the south. In extent it is slightly smaller than England, a country of mountains, deep valleys and fast-flowing rivers which flood down from the mountains to the coastal lowlands and thence to the sea. Essentially it is a very poor country. In 1870 vast sums of money were borrowed from London in order to build railways, but through incompetence and corruption most of the capital was dissipated and the country was left bankrupt and in a state of unrest. From 1883 until 1944 revolutions became a matter of course. No sooner had the Hondurans become familiar with one president than he was toppled from power and another, often very briefly, took his place.

Not that the majority of the country's some three million people have ever been interested in politics. For the most part they are of Indian stock, live in primitive conditions and are far too poor (£100 – or $250 – a year is considered a good wage) and far too busy trying to wring a meagre living from their small farms or farm-holdings to worry about what goes on in the Honduran capital of Tegucigalpa. Some breed cattle in the lowland pastures, but the country's chief product is bananas grown in large American-run plantations on the northern coastal plain and which, together with coffee, represents 50 per cent of the country's exports, the rest being made up of coconuts, timber and tobacco. It is a difficult country in which to travel because of a lack of good roads and railways and the deep valleys which cut through it like the troughs of waves (the Spanish word *honduras* may be translated as 'wavelike').

The country has two, or rather three, seasons – the wet from May to November, the dry from November to May, and September, the hurricane season. The terrible toll taken by hurricanes in the area (nearly 8,000 people lost their lives in Haiti when Hurricane Flora struck in 1963) has led countries on the Atlantic and Pacific seaboards – especially the U.S.A. – to develop meteorological services with a multiplicity of weather stations, fleets of aircraft, banks of computers and all the other trappings of modern technology to monitor the atmospheric conditions which give rise to the violent disturbances from which hurricanes are created. When one such build-up was spotted in 1974, an urgent warning went to Tegucigalpa informing the government of Honduras that it was likely to be assaulted by a hurricane within the next 48 hours. Following the obscure system then in force that bestows girls' names on hurricanes, this was given the somewhat frivolous name of 'Fifi'.

Unfortunately, communications being what they were, little could be done in the outlying districts of Honduras. Those who were informed of the danger could only wait; those who were not – and that was the bulk of the population – went about their back-breaking task of scratching a miserable living from the soil, quite oblivious to the approaching menace.

Hurricane Fifi arrived at dead of night on Wednesday, 18 September, with winds of 140 miles an hour, and torrential rain. Two feet of rain fell in 36 hours. Although the hurricane winds caused the initial damage, they soon passed and the subsequent fatalities were mainly the result of the flooding. The heavy rainfall caused the many rivers of Honduras to overflow from their sources high in the mountains right down to the plains. Dykes and banks disappeared into a maelström of swirling brown water, and almost everything that stood in the path of the floods as they roared down to the sea was swept away.

The poorly-built homes of the farmers and peasants – stone, wattle and clay for the most part – just disappeared. Even some of the sturdier houses were picked up and carried for several miles, and in some cases, when meeting an obstruction that even the roaring water could not move, would be piled one on top of another.

Worst hit was the district around the town of Choloma, standing on the banks of the river which gave it its name. Flood water poured through the town bearing trees, rocks and pathetic jumbles of wreckage that had once been homes, carrying away every standing thing along the river's bank. During the first two terrible days more than 3,000 died in the town, many of the bodies never being recovered. Those inhabitants who were left were faced with another great hazard – cholera. Bodies lay everywhere, many half-buried in the nine-feet layer of mud that the floods had left. Soon, under the hot, tropical sun, decay began to set in. Soldiers were rushed to the area and were soon collecting the bodies, piling them into heaps for mass cremation, contrary to the Roman Catholic practice of burial. Nothing, not even the deep religious beliefs of four centuries, could stand in the way of priorities.

THE HONDURAS HURRICANE

As they worked, scarves and handkerchiefs about their mouths to allay the dreadful odour of putrefaction, the pitiful survivors – about half the town's original population – stood and watched, helpless. Many, of course, had tragic stories to tell. 'People were very afraid to leave their homes,' said one survivor. 'I saw nine people from one family embrace each other; they were afraid to move. They died, holding each other in their arms.'

One old man who had lost his entire family in the flood went back to search the pile of wreckage that had been his home, and found the bodies of two dead people. He did not know them; they were not even people of Choloma. They were, as he remarked, 'just poor innocents who were swept down from the mountain and ended up here'. Another added that two separate floods had chased each other through the town early on the morning of Thursday, 19 September. 'The water poured across the street and between my home and my neighbour's like rapids.'

The second city of Honduras, San Pedro Sula, also took the full brunt of Hurricane Fifi and the floods which followed in her wake. With their homes wrecked or completely gone, some 400,000 people were suddenly homeless, without food and with the prospect of an epidemic very near.

The final death toll throughout the country was set at least at 8,000.

The first aircraft from neighbouring countries and the U.S.A. began to drone over the devastated areas, spotting thousands of terrified and desperately hungry survivors clinging to anything that protruded above the vast wastes of frothy, surging water. Some were soon saved, but the rescuers were unable to reach many of the rural areas of northern Honduras where thousands of peasants were marooned without food, fresh water or medical aid of any kind. To add to the difficulties, the only petrol refinery in the country had been isolated by the flooding of roads and the railway tracks, depriving the authorities of the fuel so vital for rescue work.

By 23 September helicopters from the U.S. base at the Panama Canal Zone were hovering wherever they could see signs of life, doubling their usual carrying capacity as they plucked wet, hungry and miserable survivors from roof-tops and trees. At first they were the only means of rescue, for bridges and railway tracks had been swept away and roads had disappeared beneath several feet of black, glutinous mud; electricity supplies were cut and telegraph-poles were down everywhere, while those that remained upright bore their pathetic bundles of squatting humanity whose upturned faces showed their mute appeal as the heavily-laden helicopters droned overhead.

As lines of communication were slowly restored, food and medical supplies began to arrive, Tocoa and San Pedro Sula becoming the main relief centres. Soon the stacks of supplies were beginning to grow, but the teams arriving from other countries ran into trouble. Corruption, always a major problem in any poor and under-developed country, became flagrant. Part of the Honduran army had been mustered to collect and distribute the food and other supplies; the rest was on guard along the Honduras/Salvador border and the government refused to bring them back and leave the border undefended. At the two main centres it was obvious that a large quantity of supplies was being diverted to a black market that had sprung into life within hours of the disaster.

Britain managed to bring some order out of the tension and even rioting at the centres. She had already sent in helicopters and troops with power-boats and medical teams from Belize in the then British Honduras, but realizing the problem was one of administration, co-ordinated all the endeavours of every assisting country through the newly-formed Whitehall Disaster Unit. This stamped out the corruption at source and helped the flow of rescue units, getting them with their supplies to the devastated areas where they were so urgently needed.

It was a prodigious task, for everywhere, it seemed, were thousands of starving people who had lost everything – corn, rice, beans and other subsistence crops having completely gone. For the country as a whole, things were even worse. With her economy utterly reliant on exports of bananas and coffee, and the plantations of these devastated, fresh crops had to be sown at once, with the prospect of at least two years wait before any return from the new plantings could be expected. Livestock had also perished in their thousands and these, too, would have to be replenished – although the country had no foreign currency available.

Only the generosity of other nations can enable Honduras to survive until she is able to return even to the near-starvation level that existed before Hurricane Fifi. Many peasants believe that the calamity was a punishment from God, but for what no-one is quite sure.

Seveso Chemical Disaster (1976)

Midway between Milan and the holiday resorts of Lake Como, the motorway cuts alongside the little Italian town of Seveso. It is a remarkably busy artery, stretching from city smog to blue skies and some of the world's most stunning scenery. During peak season, it carries tens of thousands of travellers each day.

At a passing glance, Seveso seems to be the ideal place to break the journey and stop for a meal or for petrol or simply to stretch the legs and explore. Indeed, the town first found fame for the high-class furniture produced there in workshops dotted among the picturesque homes of its friendly, generally well-to-do inhabitants.

After one curious glance, virtually all would-be sightseers do, however, pass on with a shudder and without hesitation. For Seveso, once proud of its trade and its tourism, is in the grip of a living nightmare which may never end . . .

On 10 July 1976, an explosion rocked the Icmesa chemical plant just outside town and spewed a bilious dust cloud into the air where it hung, spreading ominously above houses and farm land. Within 24 hours, vegetation downwind of the plant had begun to turn yellow. Leaves on plants and trees curled up and wilted and small animals, mysteriously, began to die. More alarmingly, young children started to develop sores on their arms and legs, red marks and rashes on their faces and high temperatures. The poison was just starting to take effect.

Doctors and officials of Icmesa, which was owned by a giant Swiss drug company, were totally baffled by the events which followed the blast at a small reactor in the factory, which produced agricultural herbicides. It was days before they realised that the explosion had produced a freak chemical 'cocktail' of Tetrachlorodibenzodioxin; more familiar to a horrified world as Agent Orange. It is the active ingredient of the defoliant used with such devastating effect by American forces in Vietnam. It was fully 10 days before the regional government declared the Seveso area polluted by dioxin. And by then it was too late.

For by then, scores of children and adults lay in hospital, their faces covered by gauze masks to hide terrible skin disorders which would leave many of them scarred for life. When the truth finally emerged, 11,000

These young sisters are being treated for skin rashes caused by the poisonous gas

townspeople fled their homes, leaving 40,000 farm animals and domestic pets to die from the effects of the poison cloud or be slaughtered. In the eerie silence of what was later named Zone A – the very heart of Seveso – barely a living thing stirred.

Within months of the disaster, which is still known as 'Italy's Hiroshima', the number of children suffering from chloracne – a persistent, dioxin-caused eruption of sore, weeping boils all over the body – had risen to 417. Five decontamination workers contracted liver disease, despite working only four-hour shifts and wearing protective clothing. And, amid fears of abnormal births, at least 400 'high risk' expectant mothers underwent abortions. One leading doctor, Paulo Bruzzi, who today maintains a still-expanding file on the health of Seveso victims, says: 'Had those children been born . . . who knows?'

Several deformities were recorded in new-born babies within months of the Icmesa factory blast, but the full toll of horror will never be known because so many fled the town when the pollution danger was discovered. Attempts to elicit information from doctors all over Italy have met with failure. In an interview in August, 1981 – five years after the nightmare began – Dr Bruzzi declared: 'There is still a danger about which we can say nothing. That is cancer. We have seen many dead animals here . . . and I have to say that if dioxin affected man as it does rabbits, Seveso would have seen a very great diseaster indeed. Yet cancer is something we cannot forget about for perhaps 10 years. We must go on watching Seveso with very great care for a very long time to come. It is too soon to ring bells of joy. The only bells to sound from Seveso must be alarms for the world.'

The Italian Government has declared that Zone A must remain closed for ever. It is a graveyard in which memories of a once-prosperous town are buried along with mounds of topsoil from less-contaminated areas – Zones B and R – and the rubble of 300 houses which were immediately demolished. A yellow fence, 10 feet high, with garish notices warning 'quarantine area' encircles the deadly core of Seveso, into which entry can only be gained with government permission for strictly limited periods, with the wearing of special protective clothing an equally strict regulation. The reason for such incredible caution is simple: no-one can be sure whether further tragedy is yet to come.

Recent tests revealed that poison levels in soil taken trom the roadside in Seveso were ten times greater than was thought. The tests, carried out by a group of Padua University professors, were rejected by the authorities as 'mistaken'. Whatever dangers do still exist, one thing is certain: the £57 million paid out in compensation by the drug firm which owned Icmesa, Hoffman La Roche, is never going to make Seveso totally safe. In an interview, one government official said: 'It is true that no-one, as far as we know, has died as a result of the poison cloud. But the fact is that we know so little about what we are dealing with. We do not know yet if we have been lucky enough.'

Just as deep-rooted as the health horrors attached to the Seveso disaster are the psychological ones which linger on. Understandably, the birth rate among those who stayed or later returned to be re-housed in 'safe areas' has plummeted. Building contractor Ugo Basilico, 45, who has a son aged 10, declares: 'Before the cloud, I had thought it was about time we had another child. But now who knows? The doctor says it is better to wait. If you have a baby with a defect, it is there for life.'

Five years after the poison cloud spread its misery, at least 193 cases of chloracne had been recorded, leaving many children scarred for life or in need of drastic cosmetic surgery. It can only be guessed how far the tragedy has spread, for a little over four months after the chemical cocktail was, inexplicably, formed and released into the atmosphere, traces of dioxin were found in the mud . . . on a street in Milan. Years of squabbling, accusations and counter-accusations by the authorities and Icmesa officials have done little to help solve the mystery.

Those years of indecision have done nothing to dull the pain or encourage hope for youngsters like little Alicia Senno, who was just four years old when the cloud of doom first overshadowed Seveso. It was a scorching-hot summer, and Alicia had been happily playing outside for days, dressed in shorts and T-shirt with her sister Stefania, aged $2\frac{1}{2}$, and other friends from the neighbourhood.

They all heard the blast. They all saw the white cloud rise. And they all played on with their toys and games. With no alarm or word of warning, they continued to run around while unknowingly exposed to the horrific poison of dioxin, now said to be the most potent known to man.

It was five days after the explosion that Alicia first fell ill. The grotesque eruptions which began to sprout all over her pretty young face came as a terrible shock to her mother and father who, along with other townspeople, had still not been fully told the extent of the dangers which had been thrown

Coal dust explosion

The world's worst mining disaster happened on 26 April 1942, when 1,572 men died in a coal dust explosion in China's Honkeiko colliery.

SEVESO CHEMICAL DISASTER

Public health department scientists gather up bags containing animal bodies

upon their community by a chemical mishap. It was only after the family was evacuated from its home that little Alicia, her sister and her mother were admitted to hospital while her father was temporarily put up at a hostel.

With a white gauze mask completely covering her face, save for slits for her eyes, nose and mouth, Alicia's condition rapidly worsened. The effects of chloracne ravaged her facial skin, leaving her in agony. As an early victim of the poison cloud, she became a human guinea-pig, being moved from hospital to hospital in Milan as doctors puzzled out how to try to deal with her appalling skin ailment.

Tissue samples were removed from her face for laboratory tests to see to what degree her skin could be regenerated. The horrendous boils did, eventually, clear up, only to re-appear again at regular intervals which is a common symptom of dioxin poisoning. At times, Alicia still has to wear that mask. It is a recurring ordeal which preys on her mind to such an extent that she is now terrified whenever a figure in white hospital uniform approaches.

Four-year-old Gianluca Bragiato was another early victim of the Seveso disaster. Months after leaving hospital, his mother still had to change the bandages which swathed his face twice a day. When visitors called at the family home, he would rush to bury his face in his father's lap to hide the shame of his disfigurement. He was terrified to show his face to jeering playmates at a nearby kindergarten and he was forced to keep well away from the sun, which made his pock-marked, scarred cheeks burn painfully. At the time of writing, young Gianluca's condition has improved considerably. Yet his doctor maintains: 'It is curable, we believe, though it may take years.'

In incredibly minute doses, measurable in parts per trillion, the chemical can kill mammals. After its widespread use as a 'forest-stripping' defoliant in Vietnam, where thousands of laid-to-waste acres are still heavily contaminated, experts came to the conclusion that in humans its effects – the extent of which are still unknown – can include, as well as chloracne and birth defects, tumours and possibly other serious disorders. Even, as is now feared, cancer.

For those who escaped the poison cloud, there was the grief of losing their homes and all their possessions. Many are adamant that no amount of compensation will ever be able to replace what they once had. Housewife Caterina Rivolta, aged 58, says: 'I would give anything to move back. All our lovely furniture is gone, as is the garden we so loved. My husband and I saved for 16 years to buy our home. Now all we can do is gaze through gaps in the fence, knowing that we cannot return. Nothing – not even any amount of money – will ever replace what we once proudly had.'

As well as the heartbreak which remains, there is still anger among the people of Seveso; anger not only over the bungles and delays which followed the explosion at Icmesa but also over the fact that nobody, not even workers at the plant, was ever warned about the potential dangers of the chemicals being handled there. Yet, who could have known that a freak reaction would result in the formation of deadly dioxin at searing temperatures of up to 158 degrees centigrade?

Still the debate rages on over what should be done to try to totally de-contaminate the area. Many experts believe that may never be possible. But others have proposed radical steps to rid the town of its nightmare. Professor Ghetti, Seveso's regional chief health officer, says: 'We should have burnt down the entire poisoned zone. What has happened here is on the same scale as Hiroshima. It is one of the most gruesome catastrophes in the world.'

Gold mine flooded
One hundred and fifty two men died when flood waters inundated the Witwatersrand gold mine in South Africa in 1909.

SEVESO CHEMICAL DISASTER

Professor Ghetti's 'solution' is, however, scoffed at by other experts, who claim that razing the contaminated areas would worsen the problem. They claim that at temperatures below 1,000 degrees centigrade, the dioxin would simply have been swept up into the air with the smoke and would, eventually, have come down somewhere else.

So the nightmare continues. Today, a crudely painted skull-and-crossbones has been daubed underneath the roadside sign which once proudly declared the name of the town Seveso. Looters and vandals, who moved in for rich and easy pickings despite exposing themselves to incredible danger shortly after the mass evacuations, have long since disappeared, as have the tourists and passing motorists whose trade once kept the town thriving. 'We used to do well from holidaymakers driving north' says the owner of a local petrol station, 'But no more. They won't even stop for gas unless they are about to run out. And as for eating here, well, would you?'

Meanwhile, in Zone A, amid the rubble-strewn poison dump which used to be the heart of Seveso, the only living things which stir are the protective-suited decontamination workers who occasionally foray into the area of devastation and desolation. No animal which ventures inside the high fence will survive for long. No bird ever sings in the town centre. For, while the human victims of Seveso are still, miraculously, alive, it is the town itself which has died.

The Tenerife Plane Crash (1977)

Tenerife is plagued by fog. Clouds bank up around the extinct volcano, Pico de Teide, and spread a sudden eerie mist across the Atlantic holiday island. On Sunday, 27 March 1977 it was very foggy.

A bomb, planted by terrorists of the Canary Islands liberation movement, had exploded in a shop at Las Palmas airport, on the neighbouring island of Gran Canaria, and aircraft were being diverted from Las Palmas to Santa Cruz. Among them were two Boeing 747 jumbo jets – Dutch KLM flight 4805 from Amsterdam and Pan Am flight 1736 from Los Angeles and New York.

The three air traffic controllers on duty in the control tower had eleven planes on the ground, all awaiting clearance for take-off. But their main concerns were the fast-thickening fog, which had reduced visibility to 500 yards, and the central runway lights, which were not working. To add to the confusion, two of the airport's three radio frequencies were out of action and the pilots had to talk to the controllers through the babble of the one remaining frequency. The scene was set for disaster.

The main east-west runway at Santa Cruz is two miles long and 2,000 feet above sea level. Parallel to it is a second runway which planes use to taxi to and from the terminal buildings. These two runways are joined at either end and are linked along their lengths by four access slipways. KLM flight 4805 and Pan Am flight 1736 were stuck in the queue on the second, 'taxi-ing' runway, the Dutch airliner just ahead of the American.

The waiting finally ended just before 5 p.m. KLM pilot Captain Jaap van Zanten announced to his 229 weary passengers that he had at last been given clearance to taxi forward in readiness for take-off to Las Palmas. Pan Am skipper Captain Victor Grubbs made a similar announcement to his 370 American passengers.

Because of the congestion on the taxi-ing runway, both pilots were ordered to move their planes on to the main runway and to taxi to the take-off starting point at the far end. The message went out from the control tower to KLM flight 4805: 'Taxi straight ahead to the end of the runway and make backtrack.'

Captain Van Zanten's mighty jet headed slowly up the long runway while

The wreckage of the Pan Am jumbo with the control tower looming behind

Captain Grubbs received his instructions from the tower – to follow the Dutch jet but to leave the runway by turning into a slipway on the left.

Captain Van Zanten completed his manoeuvre and pointed his airliner's nose into the fog that hid the two miles of main runway ahead of him. His co-pilot reported to the control tower: 'KLM 4805 is now ready for take-off. We are waiting for clearance.' The tower replied: 'OK, stand by for take-off. I will call you.'

The reason for the horrific chain of events that occurred in the next few minutes may never be discovered. What *is* known is that while the control tower was checking on the position of the Pan Am jumbo, the Dutch airliner was readying itself for take-off. And while the American plane was still lumbering up the main runway before turning off onto one of the slipways, the KLM airliner released its brakes, increased thrust and began rolling down the two miles of runway . . . straight at Pan Am flight 1736, unseen through the fog.

The Dutch jet was already travelling at 150 miles an hour when Pan Am co-pilot Robert Bragg first spotted it. He said: 'I saw lights ahead of us through the fog. At first I thought it was the KLM standing at the end of the runway. Then I realised the lights were coming towards us.' Bragg screamed: 'Get off. Get off.' Captain Grubbs shouted: 'We're on the runway. We're on the runway.'

Agonisingly slowly, Grubbs slewed his jumbo through a 30-degree turn in a last desperate attempt to avoid disaster. But it was too late. The KLM plane was travelling too fast. It could not stop or swerve. The only option for Captain Van Zanten was to try to lift the nose of his jumbo in a bid to 'hop' over the plane blocking his path.

But Captain Van Zanten had passed the point of no return. Two seconds after lifting off, the Dutch plane smashed into the American jumbo at about 160 miles an hour. The nose of the KLM jet hit the top of the other plane, taking the roof off the cockpit and the first-class upper compartment. The giant engine pods hanging beneath the wings were next to hit the American plane. The port engines ploughed into the aft-cabin, killing most of the passengers instantly.

The KLM Boeing continued its terrible journey over the top of the Pan Am plane and along the runway, disintegrating and exploding into thousands of pieces. Not one person aboard the Dutch plane survived.

All the survivors on the Pan Am plane were sitting either up front or on the left-hand side, away from the impact. Part of the left of the plane was broken off by the crash, and the survivors either were hurled clear or leaped to safety.

The crash occurred at 5.07 p.m. but throughout the long seconds of disaster, the air-traffic controllers remained unaware of it. A Spanish airliner flying above Tenerife broke in to request landing permission. The control tower replied sharply: 'Radio silence, please. I will continue to call up KLM.' But KLM no longer existed. It was a litter of blazing, scattered débris.

It was not until a gust of wind blew a gap in the fog that the controllers realised they were witnesses to the ultimate horror everyone had dreaded – a crash between two jumbo jets, each weighing 240 tons, 231 feet long and with a tailplane the height of a seven-storey building. And both crowded with passengers.

Death was instant for all 229 passengers and 15 crew of the KLM jet. But among the survivors of the Pan Am jumbo, there were tales of panic, horror and heroism.

In the first-class compartment 'all hell broke loose' according to 37-year-old passenger Jim Naik, from California. He said: 'I was sitting with my wife Elsie when there was a sudden explosion. The plane went completely up in flames. I was struggling to get Elsie out with me but after the impact people just started tumbling down on top of us from the lounge above as the ceiling caved in. A piece of ceiling fell on my wife. Then a second explosion hurled me on to the runway. I was running back towards the plane to try to save Elsie when I saw a body falling out of the plane. It was my wife.'

Californian John Amador, aged 35, said: 'I looked out of a porthole and saw the KLM plane coming right at me. I ducked and, when I looked up, our own aircraft was split into three parts. I was afraid I was going to be roasted.' But he leaped to safety.

Mrs Teri Brusco, of Oregon, said 'The Dutch jet's wings took off the whole of the top of our plane. Everyone was screaming.' Her husband Roland pushed his wife through a jagged opening in the side of the plane and they then hauled out his mother. 'My mother was on fire. We started dragging her across the field to put the flames out.'

Briton John Cooper, a 53-year-old Pan Am mechanic, was travelling as a passenger on the flight deck when the plane was hit by the KLM jumbo. He was thrown clear and suffered only minor cuts. He said: 'There was a terrible crash. I just don't want to remember it. There were people screaming terribly, women and children enveloped in flames. I will never get the sound of that screaming out of my ears.'

Explosion in Halifax harbour

Two ships collided in Halifax harbour, Nova Scotia, on 6 December 1917, and destroyed half the town. The Belgian relief ship Imo rammed the French munitions ship Mont Blanc causing a mighty explosion that killed 1,600 people, injured another 8,000 and left 2,000 listed as 'missing'. The suburb of Richmond was destroyed, rail cars were hurled more than a mile and all 200 children in an orphanage were killed. One citizen of Halifax was more lucky . . . he was hurled a mile through the air but survived after landing in a tree.

Dorothy Kelly, a 35-year-old Pan Am purser from New Hampshire, was heroine of the day. Later awarded a gallantry medal, this is what she remembered of the disaster: 'There was noise, things flying around. Nothing was recognizable. There was nothing around that looked like anything had looked before – just jagged metal and small pieces of débris. When everything settled, I realized that there was sky above me although I was still in what had been the aircraft. At first, I didn't see any people at all. There were explosions behind me and I realized that the only way out was up. The floor started giving way as I climbed out.'

Mrs Kelly leaped 20 feet to safety then looked back at the broken and blazing plane. There was a string of explosions and she heard people screaming from within the aircraft – so she ran back towards it.

'I saw the captain on his knees, not moving. I thought he had broken his legs. There were other people around with broken limbs. I grabbed the captain under the arms and pulled and kept encouraging him to keep going. I feared the fuselage would fall down on us. There was a huge explosion. I said: "We've got to move faster." I kept pushing and pulling and then dropped him on to the runway.'

Having saved the life of Captain Grubbs, Mrs Kelly dashed back and forth, dragging other dazed survivors clear of the wreckage until she was certain that there could be no one else left alive.

But explosions were ripping through the jumbo. A final series of blasts engulfed the plane in flames. There was no longer any hope of survival for anyone left aboard. Of the 370 passengers and 16 crew of the jumbo, more than 300 were dead within minutes of the crash and more than 60 were seriously injured. The final death toll on the day the two leviathans of the skies collided was a horrifying 582.

The Big Heat
(1980)

The Big Heat began in June, scoring out a vast, arid dust bowl across thousands of miles of land. Farmers faced ruin as their animals died and their crops were destroyed. Even the super-rich cattle ranchers of the mid-West saw fortunes wiped out. But the Big Heat came to cost more than dollars. It cost lives, on an incredible scale . . .

Summer 1980 saw a trail of disaster sweep across America as the highest temperatures ever recorded in the country turned life into a red-hot hell. Twenty states were hit hard by the killer heatwave and, within a month of the weather going wild on 22 June, at least 1,200 people had died. Old folk simply collapsed in the street. The crime rate soared as people were driven into a frenzy as the sun burned down. And, as youngsters were forced to stay indoors, cases of child abuse rocketed as family frustrations boiled over.

The mid-West and Southern states were worst affected. Dallas, Texas, bore the brunt of the Big Heat with an astonishing 23 consecutive days of temperatures in excess of 100 degrees farenheit. Carole Bowdry, the city's Director of a Child Abuse Prevention Program, had to admit: 'In the past few weeks, my caseload has been up substantially. It is becoming a terrible problem. If you're hot, you're going to get angry faster. If the parents are the type who are going to be abusive, this is the time when it will show up.' In Missouri, one tragic victim was a two-year-old boy, who died after two hours locked in a van parked in the street. He had been put there because his mother could not find a baby-sitter.

One of the most gruesome stories to emerge from the heatwave nightmare involved a band of illegal aliens from El Salvador, who had been smuggled across the border, en masse, from Mexico into Arizona. Of the 26 back-door immigrants who made what in normal circumstances would have been a hazardous journey, only 13 ever arrived. The rest died under a cruel, blazing sun.

The ages of victims in the worst-hit states ranged from six months to 90; no-one escaped the merciless melting-pot.

Raging brush fires, sparked on bone-dry, tinder-box land, swept Arizona. Part of a highway in Okemah, Oklahoma literally blew-up, scattering chunks of concrete as effectively as if it had been dynamited. In Macon, Georgia, the city's air-conditioned Coliseum had to be opened up as an emergency refuge for people in distress. By early July, the weathermen were predicting worse to come.

Extreme temperatures were accompanied by incredibly high humidity, picked up from the Gulf of Mexico, which made it almost impossible to stay out of doors for any length of time without contracting heatstroke. From state to state, governors were declaring emergency zones and setting up relief centres. In Washington, President Carter ordered the release of almost 7 million dollars in emergency federal funds to assist in 'heat relief' programmes. That cash aid brought little relief, however, to farmers whose losses by then had been conservatively estimated at a staggering 2,000 million dollars.

For the cattle men of Kansas the drought caused by the Big Heat was particularly ruinous. During one market day at the height of the freak weather in the small town of Hutchinson, 40 miles north-west of Wichita, Joe Thaxton, a part-owner of the market, stood in the shade of a tree, pushed his blue peak cap above his sweat-beaded forehead and told newsmen who had gathered to witness the death of a community: 'They're being forced to bring the cattle in one-and-a-half months early. They don't have no grass in the fields and they can't afford the price of cattle feed. So they have to sell; they don't have no choice. We're getting 30 per cent more to sell than we usually get at this time of the year and the prices are way down. If we don't get a good rain soon, 15 per cent of the farmers will go bankrupt. It will be a total disaster.'

Swiftly, the price of hay rocketed so high that farmers were unable to afford to feed their livestock. Ranchers were forced to make the agonizing choice of either borrowing heavily to afford foodstuffs which had more than doubled in price – or slaughter their cattle. Crops were decimated and in many areas the poultry industry was savagely hit. Corn, soya beans, green vegetables and fruit were all ruined. In Arkansas, America's main producer of chickens, the birds perished in the sizzling heat and many thousands had to be slaughtered.

The crippling, natural disaster could not have come at a worse time for the country's beleaguered farmers who were already facing deep financial trouble because of a combination of inflation, the recession and a Government ordered embargo on grain exports to the Soviet Union. According to one report in the British *Guardian* newspaper: 'Flying into Wichita provides a graphic overview of parched, brown fields shorn of grass or dotted with stunted crops. Each morning at dawn, the sun comes up as a bright red ball over the flat plain, signalling another day of unremitting heat.'

Bryce Owr, the county's agricultural agent, put the disaster into enlightening perspective when he told the newspaper: 'My father was a farmer. It hurt; but we had enough to get by on. In those days we were in the Depression and nobody had nothing, so your demands were not that great.

THE BIG HEAT

A young heat victim being treated in Houston

It can happen again. We have only been in the heat for a few weeks. But since it began, we have learned a lot about conservation. They have planted wind-breakers – trees and shrubs – and reservoirs have been made and a lot of land has been put back to grass. That binds it and stops it going to dust. We have learned a lot . . .'

The parallel with Depression-era America was especially poignant, for the scorching temperatures of summer 1980 topped even those of the worst previous heatwave of the mid-1930s, in which about 15,000 people are estimated to have died during three terrible years. Then, people took to sleeping on benches in public parks during the long, hot nights. In 1980, anyone who had dared to do that would have left themselves a sitting target

Horrific drought

Australia, facing rationing and hardship after years of war was, in 1944–45, hit by a disastrous drought. The harvest failed and the number of sheep in Australia fell by more than a third. It took 10 years for the sheep stocks to recover their original levels.

for the muggers and molesters whose trade in violence had been accelerated by the steam-bath conditions.

Across the sweltering states, night time temperatures often only dipped as far as the mid to high eighties. In towns across the country, where the Red Cross was busy distributing free fans and opening air-conditioned emergency centres, people were bringing their beds onto their porches or on to the strips of brown grass at the fronts and backs of their homes. Bars and restaurants did not report the expected sharp rise in demand for cold drinks – people just could not summon up the energy to leave their houses. One resident told journalists: 'The thought of food and cooking just repels me. I just want to sit at home in the cool. After a day's work you feel totally drained.' Needless to say, as the crime boom continued, there was a massive surge in the number of thefts of air-conditioning units. Demand for electricity also rose as millions of desperate inhabitants switched on all available air-conditioning in their search for at least a degree of relief.

For many, there was none. The death toll was highest in the poorer areas, where many people did not have air-conditioning. By 21 July, the people of Kansas were celebrating the fact that the mercury was registering a mere 93 degrees farenheit. It was only the second day in a month that it had not reached three figures, the peak of which was an almost unbelievably stifling 114 degrees. On one night in Washington, the temperature did not fall below 91 degrees, with a relative humidity of 85 per cent – the equivalent of a turkish bath.

Miners trapped

A coal mine disaster at Courrières, northern France, in 1906 killed more than 1,000 pitmen. The surviving miners, trapped far below ground, lost all sense of time. When rescued, they thought they had been incarcerated for four to five days. In fact, they had been underground for three weeks.

THE BIG HEAT

The Big Heat did bring to the simmering surface several stories of a rather more humanly quirky nature. In almost a double-take of the song about 'Mad dogs and Englishmen', hoteliers in Florida watched in utter amazement as thousands of British holidaymakers on cheap package tours went out to fry themselves on the beaches in the midday sun. One Palm Beach hotel owner declared incredulously: 'They are out there every day, lying on the beach or walking along the baking streets . . . even when the sun is at its height.' California, on the other hand, was in the grip of a new craze; people were spending a fortune visiting solariums for daily three-minute sessions under sun lamps to maintain their tans!

American industry suffered badly as the Big Heat continued to bite through July. Hundreds of companies were rocked by absenteeism as workers simply shut themselves indoors to escape the sun's piercing rays. Hospital staffs across the country were stretched to the limit treating sunstroke cases. One Dallas hospital alone treated thousands of sun-affected patients in little over a fortnight.

It seemed as if it would never end. Virtually every facet of private and public life took a blistering from the Big Heat. But the solar onslaught did subside and the rains did come. From the heatbowl of July, August began with cooler temperatures and almost as suddenly as it had all begun, nature seemed to return to normal . . . having left a trail of death and destruction in the wake of almost two months during which the sun went wild. The Big Heat was over.

North Sea Oil Rig Disaster (1980)

A mocking cheer of sympathy went echoing round the cinema as movie star Robert Redford appeared on screen, tugging a crude fur coat round his face to cover himself against the biting, snow-laden winds.

The all male audience in the private cinema were thoroughly enjoying Redford's performance as 'Jeremiah Johnson', a tough frontiersman fighting for his life in a desolate Rocky Mountain wilderness. The audience knew a thing or two about survival in the face of Nature's fury. They considered themselves experts.

On the flickering screen, a raging storm forced 'Jeremiah' to huddle deeper inside his makeshift shelter of branches and twigs. Outside the cinema a real-life gale, with winds of 70 miles an hour, battered against the double glazed windows, adding its own howling to the film's sound track.

The 100 seat cinema was at near capacity. Across a narrow corridor, on the same level, a staff of six were busy preparing the menu for an evening meal offering a choice of steak or fresh salmon. The adjoining restaurant already had a small group of customers starting on their first course of thick chicken broth and freshly baked rolls. In the accommodation block, one floor above the cinema, some men were lounging on their beds, watching television or writing letters to sweethearts, wives and children.

Slowly at first, the cinema began to shake and rock. It had happened before. There was no alarm, only some muttered curses from the audience as drinks began to spill over their tables and ashtrays tumbled to the floor. Gradually the cinema floor levelled itself again and a few of the men got to their feet, wiping cigarette ash and drinks from their trousers.

Then the floor began to tilt again, this time steeper and steeper. Tables began to slip towards the rear wall. Those men on their feet clutched unsteadily at the bar for support, until the counter wrenched itself slowly from the brackets holding it to the floor. There was a groaning sound of twisting metal as the angle of the floor increased, then a sudden explosive bang. The first fearful shouts came as the floor lurched at a crazy angle and men dropped to their knees, trying vainly to dig their fingernails into the thick carpet to prevent themselves sliding into the jumble of furniture and bodies piling up against the rear wall.

NORTH SEA OIL RIG DISASTER

A heavy trestle table tumbled end over end across the cinema, smashing through a window and allowing a sudden blast of bitterly cold wind into the room, blowing curtains, table cloths and cushions into a miniature whirlwind.

On the cinema screen, tilted at an angle of 25 degrees, actor Robert Redford huddled over a camp fire and prepared to skin and cook a deer. His image began to shake, the moving pictures slipping from the white screen. Redford's distorted face appeared briefly on the ceiling before the projector at the rear of the cinema broke free of its mountings and crashed into the wall.

One heavy chair slid along the wall and wedged itself in the emergency door as some of the men clawed their way along the carpet towards safety. For a few moments they tugged at the chair, then the emergency exit flew open. But the sudden movement of the door had not been the result of their frantic efforts, it had been struck on the outside by drums of oil tumbling down the corridor. Black waves of oil flooded into the cinema and the men who had almost reached freedom slid helplessly back into one sinking corner.

Ten seconds later, the cinema, the sleeping quarters, the restaurant and hospital and the whole complex of buildings on the deck of the Alexander Kielland oil platform accommodation rig, toppled 100 feet into the raging waters of the North Sea.

Two hundred and thirteen men – Norwegians, Americans and Britons, some of the toughest North Sea oil roustabouts, had been relaxing on board the supply rig that night, 27 March 1980. Their temporary home had been the 10,105 ton semi-submersible oil rig, once an active North Sea drilling and exploring platform, now converted into a floating hotel.

Even with surface waves of 30 or 40 feet, as they were that stormy March night, the rig should only have bobbed up and down by three or four feet, its steel legs half filled with water acting as stabilising ballast.

Although the Alexander Kielland's exploration days were over, the rig still supported a top heavy 200 ton drilling tower which her owners, the Stavanger Drilling Company of Norway, had not dismantled. But the rig had undergone other modifications. It had been adapted to carry a three storey accommodation block, providing a home, entertainment and medical facilities for 350 men.

The rig's new job was to move from site to site in the Norwegian sector of the North Sea oil fields, acting as a mobile depot providing a work force for other rigs which were in fixed production positions. The men of the Alexander Kielland would work for a few weeks at a time alongside new production rigs, and would then be towed to another site inside the Ekofisk

NORTH SEA OIL RIG DISASTER

A crew accommodation platform

oilfield, halfway between the coasts of Norway and Scotland.

There was one other modification to the original design of the Alexander Kielland. Each of the rig's five legs was strengthened by tubular steel braces, hollow struts of one and a quarter inch steel. A ten-inch circular hole had been cut in one of the braces to install a hydrophone, an electronic listening device which would allow the Alexander Kielland to manoeuvre itself accurately into position above a beacon placed on the ocean bed. The hole, a mere pinprick in the awesome web of the rig's metalwork, had been casually sealed and then simply welded.

On the night of the disaster, the Alexander Kielland was on hire to the Phillips Petroleum Company and was stationed 150 miles off the Norwegian coast, rising and falling in the gathering storm alongside the production rig Edda. A 100-feet long flexible catwalk connected the Kielland and the Edda. While the Edda stood firmly with its own feet planted on the ocean bed, ten strong sea anchors, attached two at a time to each of the Alexander Kielland's legs, kept the 'floatel' in position beside the production rig.

As the wind and waves began to batter both platforms, senior oil technicians considered moving the Alexander Kielland further away from the Edda platform in case the floating rig dragged her anchors and scraped alongside the Edda. But the Alexander Kielland had ridden out bigger storms than the one blowing that night.

NORTH SEA OIL RIG DISASTER

The Alexander Kielland's anchors were holding fast. The 'floatel' was a rugged construction and her certificate of seaworthiness had been renewed only a month earlier by an insurance inspection agency whose engineers assured them that the four-year-old platform was in first class structural condition.

As night fell, no-one noticed the gaping cracks which began to spread along the 'pinprick' in the bracing strut as the waves pounded the Alexander Kielland. Shortly after 6.30 p.m., twisted and buckled by the forces of the ocean, the bracing strut gave way without warning and one of the giant supporting legs, immediately beneath the accommodation block, began to rip itself away from the platform.

Chief steward Thomas Greenwood of Keighley, West Yorkshire, was in the kitchen helping to prepare the evening meal, when the platform began to tilt wildly. He said later:

'The first thing I felt was a shudder, then the screeching of metal. I thought perhaps the derrick crane on the edge of the platform, used for lifting stores on board, was beginning to collapse. Then the whole kitchen began to tilt over. Pots and pans started to slide off the shelves and I heard pandemonium breaking out in the mess restaurant next door where plates were falling off tables and the furniture was beginning to topple over.

The men from the mess were dragging their way along the corridor as the platform went over at an angle of about 30 degrees and we all began pulling ourselves along the handrail towards the control room at the end of the corridor, the highest part of the rig. We had almost reached the control room when a river of oil from the busted drums on deck came gushing down the corridor and we all slipped back about 50 feet.

I found a way out halfway down the corridor and pulled myself on to the helicopter landing pad. I braced myself beside a window and helped to pull four or five people out and throw them towards the lifeboat. The last man was trying to climb up the gangway as the platform began to fall more steeply into the sea. He had almost made it when a blue gas cylinder broke loose from a shelf on the gangway and hit him. He just disappeared out of sight.'

On the sloping platform, now almost vertical, four men were killed when a 300-ton piece of machinery, a massive blow-out preventer valve, was ripped from its housing and smashed them into the sea. Greenwood, 37, found that the rig had tilted over so far that its lifeboats were entangled in the platform structure and he bravely managed to winch one of them down to the sea, 100 feet below. Then he set himself the task of trying to help the pathetic band of survivors closest to him.

Two men, numbed with cold, hung limply from metal railings on the platform, their lifejackets firmly caught. The steward cut one free with his penknife, watching the man drop into the waves and get carried towards the lifeboat. He tore the other man free and waited for a big wave to sweep towards them. Then he dropped him.

'He screamed all the way down to the water' Greenwood said. 'Then he was washed out behind the other man. I was hanging on to one edge of the platform, watching her going slowly over. At the far end I could see the accommodation unit, with the lads inside trying to smash the windows to get out. It was horrifying. When the rig became horizontal, the water and waves began to force their way into the accommodation and enormous pressure built up in the rooms and corridors. Then the windows started to blow out under the pressure. Lifejackets, quilts, mattresses and bodies were all blown out into the sea. I'll never forget that sight.'

When Greenwood finally threw himself into the water, he struck out for a lifeboat and spent the night afloat with 27 other survivors before a helicopter rescued them at dawn next day.

Oil company representative Ronald Jackson, 39, from Manchester, was one of the audience in the cinema when the rig began to tilt. 'All the chairs and bottles were just sliding along the floor' he recalled. 'They crashed into the movie screen and the water flooded through the windows and people just disappeared underneath. I panicked like mad when I saw electric cables burning and sparking outside the cinema just before the power failed. I made it to the deck but it was nearly impossible to climb in the dark. It was at 45 degrees by that time. Steel ropes were flying about, drums of oil were bursting open everywhere and the water level was rising. It was like a crazy nightmare.'

Jackson was thrown clear and struggled to a lifeboat.

Aboard the production platform Edda, only 30 yards away, the crew watched in stunned horror as the Alexander Kielland tipped most of the living souls aboard her into the surging waves. Many of the men on the Edda had been preparing to finish their working shift and getting ready to struggle back along the flexible catwalk to the Alexander Kielland for the hot meal,

---

Yachtsmen die

Fifteen yachtsmen died in August 1979, when appalling sea conditions hit the three-day race from Cowes, Isle of Wight, to the Fastnet Rock, off southern Eire. Twenty five of the competing boats sank and 19 more were abandoned in a Force 11 Atlantic gale. Only 90 of the 300 competing boats finished.

the comfort of the cinema and the safe luxury of a warm bed they believed awaited them.

As the first frantic Mayday radio messages filled the airwaves, the production crew of the Edda desperately lined the edge of their platform, ripping off their own lifejackets and throwing them to the drowning men in the water. The temperature in the North Sea that night was four degrees above freezing. No-one without a specially insulated survival suit could live more than 10 minutes before they died of exposure.

Only a pitiful few of the screaming men in the water managed to swim the short gap between the sinking 'floatel' and the production platform. The men of the Edda lowered ropes and baskets and winched down their own two lifeboats as they watched struggling survivors being dashed to their deaths in waves which slammed them into the twisted metalwork of the Alexander Kielland and the solid legs of the Edda.

Within minutes of the radio alert, the shore based rescue services had scrambled into action. As Sea King helicopters of the Royal Air Force at Boulmer, 180 miles away on the Northumberland coast, and the helicopters of the Royal Norwegian Air Force at Stavanger, roared into the air, a small flotilla of trawlers and supply ships were ordered to the scene of the disaster.

Two hours after take-off, Rescue 31, a Sea King of A Flight, 202 Squadron, Royal Air Force, hovered over the stricken platform, only 30 feet above the wave tops. Co-pilot Flight Lieutenant Michael Lakey was first to spot the bobbing liferaft with ten survivors aboard, men who had escaped the horror of the Alexander Kielland but who were already beginning to weaken and die of exposure in their liferaft.

Lakey reported: 'The sea was so rough that at first we thought it would be better to direct a surface rescue vessel to the liferaft rather than try to winch the survivors up ourselves. Then we realized this would take too long.'

Swooping down above the crashing seas, winchman Flight Sergeant Michael Yarwood lowered himself towards the life raft. Time after time he tried to get aboard the raft but the pounding waves smashed the raft against him, leaving his legs battered and bleeding. Yarwood realized he had only one chance to save the dying men. As one surging wave swept towards him out of the darkness, he unhooked his own safety lifeline and 'surfed' along the crest of the wave until he grabbed the edge of the raft. Then he guided the helicopter overhead and one by one the men were lifted to safety and dropped aboard the helicopter pad of the oil rig Edda.

A new danger for the flying rescue teams rolled in on the freezing night air – a thick sea mist enveloping and obscuring the wave tops. Frustrated by the fog and unable to see the surface of the water with their powerful searchlights, the crew of Rescue 31 reluctantly climbed to a safe height of

The enormous broken-off leg of the capsized platform is examined by experts

2,000 feet to avoid the danger of ditching in the water or colliding with the Edda rig or other search aircraft. The enforced climb probably saved the lives of more than a score of Kielland survivors. At 2,000 feet Rescue 31 clearly picked up the bleeping signal of an automatic distress beacon. Homing in on the beacon in the misty blackness, they found a lifeboat with 26 exhausted and injured men aboard.

Again Flight Sergeant Yarwood was winched down into the ocean. He reported back that the lifeboat was not badly damaged and that none of the occupants were seriously injured. Unable to lift all the men off, the Sea King stayed hovering protectively above their frail lifeboat, radioing their precise position until a rescue tug reached the survivors. As the fog thickened around the Ekofisk oilfield, Rescue 31 flew 30 miles to an oil rig in the Auk field for re-fuelling and waited for dawn to resume the search.

First light brought an eerie calm to the North Sea. The distinctive silhouette of the Alexander Kielland had disappeared forever from the skyline. Clearly visible above the sea were four of the 'feet' of the platform. Half a mile away the swell was breaking over the drifting remains of the fifth leg, the main support which had been positioned below the corner of the platform holding the accommodation block.

The Alexander Kielland had turned completely upside down. Eighty-nine men had been rescued, fifty bodies had been recovered and seventy-three were still missing.

The capsized platform was firmly tethered between the Norwegian tugs and salvage vessels and divers plunged into the icy water, hoping desperately to find men trapped among air pockets in the twisted wreckage. Trying to keep their own air supply hoses from becoming entangled, the divers began to feel their way down the hollow legs, hammering them furiously with metal bars, waiting for any feeble reply. They got no answers.

As major support ships arrived in the Ekofisk oilfield, more divers with powerful lights and underwater cutting equipment were sent 200 feet down into the silent upside-down world of the Alexander Kielland. They were confronted by a bizarre scene.

Peeping through the maze of corridors in the accommodation block, they reported overhead lighting below them and carpeted floors above. In the kitchen many of the ovens and sinks were still firmly secured to the 'ceiling'. The divers were ordered not to penetrate into the interior of the platform. They attached strong steel ropes to the Alexander Kielland to begin the long job of towing her back to the sheltered Norwegian fiords where a long detailed examination of the floating inverted wreck could be made.

Salvage experts knew that moving the upturned platform away from the scene would be a risky job. They feared that the superstructure of the platform might drag along the ocean bed and rupture one of the intricate network of North Sea oil and gas pipelines, causing a disastrous blowout. The divers and submarines were sent to the ocean floor to check if the Alexander Kielland and her overturned drilling derrick had enough clearance to tow her over the top of the Ekofisk pipelines.

The North Sea oilmen watched a grim underwater vista relayed to them from the ocean floor as they sat in the floating control rooms of their salvage ships, hunched before their television monitors. As the ocean bed came into focus they saw with some relief that the Alexander Kielland's 100 foot drilling derrick had sheared clean off and was lying on its side, no longer pointing straight down from the platform and no longer a threat to the triangle of pipelines just a few hundred yards away. The mass of ropes, cables and ladders hanging from the upturned platform made it extremely dangerous for any divers to approach too close.

The salvage controllers were ordering the cameras to give them close-up pictures of the drilling derrick when they caught the first glimpse of some of the men who had lost their lives. Even the hard-bitten oilmen were stunned and shocked by what they saw.

The bodies were entagled in the cables, some of them lay on the ocean floor, draped lifelessly across the oil pipeline they had worked so hard to lay and service. Some were clad only in jeans and t-shirts, lying still among the wreckage of the furniture from the Alexander Kielland's cinema. Others were in pyjamas and dressing gowns, trapped without warning and drowned in their bedrooms when their floating hotel had hit the waves and filled with water.

A day later the ocean-going tugs took up the slack on the steel hawsers attached to the Alexander Kielland and began the sombre journey towards the sheltered deep water of Stavenger Fiord. Over the next seven days, as the ghostly platform was towed underwater back to its homeland, 20 more bodies were recovered from the cold water of the Ekofisk oilfield.

In the North Sea, where death is never far away, the oil rig workers went about their daily business of capturing the riches under the ocean floor for an energy hungry world. Rewarded by salaries of up to £1,000 a week they suppressed their fears and waited for the engineers' reports to tell them why the Alexander Kielland had turned from a floating haven into a watery grave.

In London and Stavanger, committees of insurance brokers sat down to carve up the responsibility for footing the £30 million insurance loss for the Alexander Kielland and to choose a salvage contractor to try to coax more than 10,000 tons of steel, standing on its head, back on to its feet.

At R.A.F. Boulmer, gallantry awards were bestowed on the crew of Sea

NORTH SEA OIL RIG DISASTER

King helicopter Rescue 31. The Air Force Cross was awarded to pilot Flight Lieutenant Robert Edward Neville who displayed 'the highest standards of flying skill and leadership'. The Queen's Commendation went to Flight Lieutenant Michael Lakey and winch operator Flight Sergeant John Moody. Winchman Flight Sergeant Michael Yarwood was honoured with the Air Force Medal, praised for his 'outstanding courage, professional skill and pertinancity'.

A year after the disaster, the Norwegian Government inquiry concluded that modifications to the bracing strut of the Alexander Kielland had weakened the metal. They criticised the design and servicing of the platform, pointing out that the lifeboat launching mechanism had failed to operate and three of the Alexander Kielland's lifeboats had been smashed to pieces on the sides of the platform.

They described the emergency precautions as 'abysmal' and the safety checks as 'inadequate'. And they revealed that out of the 212 men on board only 76 of them had attended a safety course.

Perhaps this appalling tragedy, the worst of its kind, could have been avoided.

The Las Vegas MGM Fire (1980)

Las Vegas was the glittering gambling centre of the world, a neon-lit oasis in the Nevada desert that existed only for fun. First settled only in 1905, it was a mining community of just over 8,000 people until the 1950s, when favourable state gaming laws turned it, almost overnight, into a mecca for everyone chasing a get-rich-quick dream. Skyscraper hotels featuring lush casinos and floor shows studded with the top international stars mushroomed along the legendary Strip, luring gamblers from all over the globe to lose their money in fruit machines that offered a million dollar payout for a ten dollar stake. The rich and would-be rich flocked to the city without clocks to pursue their fortunes in a gaudy, unreal world.

But at 7.15 a.m. on the morning of 21 November 1980, cruel reality turned the tinsel dream into a nightmare. One of the worst hotel fires in America's history left 84 people dead, more than 600 others injured.

The Grand Hotel had been opened on the Strip by Hollywood film-makers MGM in 1973. It cost £50 million, had 2,100 bedrooms, and was named after the company's successful Thirties film starring Greta Garbo. Singing stars such as Tom Jones and Englebert Humperdinck earned up to £125,000 a week from cabaret sessions in the vast gambling saloon on the first of the hotel's 26 storeys. That saloon had shared in a bumper take for Nevada casinos in 1979 – an estimated $2,100,000,000. The odds were that 1980 would be even more profitable.

Then came the disaster of 21 November. It began when cooking fat in the basement kitchen which served the hotel's five restaurants overheated, and set fire to the ceiling. In seconds, a horrific fireball had built up and burst into the 140 feet long casino, one of the biggest in the world. Even at 7.15 a.m., it was still crowded with gamblers, be-jewelled and be-furred women playing the blackjack tables, dinner-suited men feeding dollars into the 1,000 slot machines. Ten of the gamblers died where they sat. Others seemed stunned, staring motionless at the roaring flames. 'Within 90 seconds, the entire casino had been engulfed', a card dealer recalled later.

Casino staff were among the first to react. Girl croupiers grabbed cash drawers and raced for the exits. Dealers dashed for the doors, cramming betting chips into their pockets as they ran. Security guards scooped up armfuls of dollar bills and dropped them into a fireproof vault before

Smoke pours from the MGM Grand Hotel at the height of the fire

escaping. Flames pursued the fleeing gamblers through the doors, blowing up two cars outside. Inside, a huge electronic Keno board, used for a bingo-style betting game, exploded and fuelled the fire, which fed hungrily on plastic fittings, flock wallpaper, plush carpets and synthetic furnishings. Gaping openings in the hotel walls, where construction work was in progress, created a convection effect, and breezes through windows broken by panicking gamblers also fanned the flames. But now an even more deadly menace emerged.

The burning furnishings and carpets gave off noxious gases, clouds of thick, choking, yellow-brown smoke which mushroomed up the staircases and lift shafts to the upper storeys of the building, where more than 1,000 guests were sleeping, unaware of the drama downstairs. None of the mirror-ceiling bedrooms had smoke detectors and, amazingly, no alarm was sounded. Fire chiefs said later that amplification systems burnt out before the sirens had a chance to blare. Some fire doors had been left open, which filled corridors with the creeping, suffocating blanket of fumes. Tragically, others had been left locked – a factor which was to cost several lives.

The first warning most sleepers had of their peril was the approaching din of fire-engines and ambulances as the Las Vegas emergency services swung into action. Then US Air Force helicopters arrived around the top floor of the skyscraper, urging people through loud-hailers to climb on to the roof to be rescued. A fleet of 12 choppers winched them up, landing them on the car park below. But some guests never made it. A rescue team led by Dr Phil Taylor later found 18 asphyxiated bodies on one staircase, huddled together in terror after finding themselves trapped between an impenetrable wall of smoke and a jammed door.

Panic and confusion set in, especially when those at the top of the building saw that the ladders of the 30 fire-engines ringing the hotel could reach only the ninth floor. Guests opened their room doors to be met with choking fumes. Many could not open their windows because of anti-suicide safety catches. They had to smash the glass to reach their balconies.

'People were screaming and throwing furniture through windows and begging to be saved,' said county fire chief Ralph Dinsman. The lucky ones scrambled down scaffolding hastily erected by workmen from a nearby building site, or were carried to safety on the hotel's exterior window-cleaning lift. Others could not wait for rescue. A desperate, half-choked woman flung herself to her death from a 17th floor balcony. Two men trying to climb from their sixth floor room also plunged to the ground and were killed.

Police with loud-hailers pleaded with guests at the upper windows not to try to clamber down the steep sides of the building. But many defied the warning – and lived to tell the tale. Donna Gleave, a survivor from the 20th floor, said: 'A man lowered his wife down from the 21st floor on a rope made from bed sheets, and I pulled her in at my window. Then we lowered ourselves to the 19th and were rescued.'

Two British businessmen escaped because their automatic alarm clock went off too early by mistake. Roy Taylor, events manager at the National Exhibition Centre in Birmingham, and David McAllister, from Aldershot, Hampshire, had a room on the sixth floor. Mr Taylor, 40, said: 'We'd forgotten to switch the clock off and it rang at 6.40. I turned it off and we were just going back to sleep when David mumbled about smelling something burning. We opened the bedroom door and were knocked back by a wall of smoke. We tried to open the window, but there were catches designed to stop people falling out. We hurled a coffee table through the glass then dropped mattresses and bedding on to a flat roof three floors 40 feet below. David hung by his hands from the sill, then dropped. I was about to do the same when he shouted, "Go back." I ducked as a shower of glass

A U.S. Air Force helicopter lifts a hotel guest to safety

cascaded down from above. It would have sliced my head off. Then I jumped. We were met by firemen who took us down smoke-filled stairs.'

British holidaymakers Russell and Lilian Ireland, from Ealing, West London, also battled their way out of the deathtrap. They were up early because they were due to check out and fly home. Then they heard sirens and smoke began pouring into their sixth floor room. 'There were no alarms, no sprinklers, and no directions to the fire escapes,' said Mr Ireland, 59. 'I grabbed Lilian and told two other women to follow us. The fire door was locked but we managed to tear the damn thing open. It was a hell of a difficult job.'

Up on the 22nd floor, James Mackey and his wife, from Michigan, learned what was happening from a radio newsflash. 'We put mattresses against the wall and stuffed towels under the door,' he said. 'We put a note on the door and prayed a lot.' Firemen rescued them.

Five floors below, Keith Breverton opened his door to find 'an impassable hell.' He said later: 'It was death, absolute death out there. People were screaming, "What shall we do?"'. Mr Breverton slammed the door shut, and lay on the floor to escape the worst of the smoke. Convinced he was about to die, he hastily scribbled notes on the only paper available – the backs of cheques. Firemen who found him unconscious revived him with oxygen before lowering him to safety.

As in the case of the 1974 Sao Paulo fire in Brazil, the horrific scenes resembled the Steve McQueen movie, *The Towering Inferno*. And following the example set in the film saved more than one Las Vegas guest. Greg Williams told reporters: 'I'd seen the film. I wrapped a wet towel round my head, got down on my hands and knees and crawled under the smoke to a fire exit.'

Outside, in the chill morning air, dazed guests wandered in the 43-acre grounds of the hotel, some barefoot and weeping, still in their nightclothes after a late night in the casino, some with fur coats draped over negligees. On the street a doctor pounded the heart of a man who had collapsed and a grim-faced priest moved among the injured waiting for an ambulance, absolving those least likely to make it. Again and again, rescue teams plunged into the blackened building after fresh alerts – people were trapped in the lifts, staff counting the multi-million takings in a locked room were unaccounted for.

After two hours, firemen had controlled the flames on the lower floors. Masked men edged upwards through the smoke to continue the grisly job of retrieving bodies. A construction worker stumbled over a huddled group in the pitch-dark casino. A waiter was found beside the tray on which he had been serving breakfast. Two guests were discovered, choked to death, in their rooms. Others were found where they had fallen in smoke-filled

Hurricane Camille

Holidaymakers at the luxurious Richelieu Apartments in Pass Christian, Mississippi, decided to hold a party and watch the storm after warnings that Hurricane Camille was heading for the American Gulf Coast on Sunday, 17 August 1969. Twenty six of them died when winds racing at 200 miles per hour smashed the apartments to pieces, and virtually wiped out the town. Camille, described by Dr Robert Simpson, director of Florida's National Hurricane Shelter as 'the greatest recorded storm ever to hit a populated area in the Western Hemisphere', spread devastation across a 70-mile swathe of Mississippi, Louisiana and Alabama. A total of more than 250 men, women and children died, 130 of them in the Mississippi town of Gulfport. Nearly 19,500 homes and 700 small businesses were demolished, and three large cargo ships were torn from their moorings and beached. The death toll might have been higher, had 150,000 people not had more sense than the Pass Christian revellers – they fled away from the coast before the hurricane arrived.

staircases. Amazingly, one guest was found alive in her room several hours after the fire was out. Firemen said she was 'just too afraid to come out'.

As the smouldering hotel was damped down and closed up, the questions began. Why was no alarm sounded? Why were there automatic sprinkler systems on only the bottom three floors? Why were there no smoke detectors in the bedrooms? Why were so many staircase doors locked, trapping many who might have escaped the disaster? Hotel president Bernard Rothkopf insisted that the building was not in breach of any building or fire safety codes, and he was backed by security expert Don Busser, who said: 'You cannot blame MGM management entirely, the state bears some responsibility.' He said the Grand had been completed to 1970 fire code standards. Though stringent new regulations had been introduced in 1979, they applied only to new buildings. Fire chief Dinsman admitted that no government agency had ever conducted a fire drill in any of the Las Vegas skyscrapers.

MGM Hotel Corporation stock slumped on the share markets as law suits on behalf of those killed or injured poured in. A total of 429 claims were filed, demanding almost two billion dollars in compensation and punitive damages. The tragedy also heralded a crisis for the whole of Las Vegas. It came just three months after thousands of gamblers were evacuated from a casino in nearby Lake Tahoe after a 1,000 lb bomb was planted. And it was followed, over the next five months, by three other hotel blazes in Vegas.

Sixteen people were hurt when fire broke out on the fifth floor of Caesar's Palace in April 1981, and in February, eight people died and 300 were hurt when four separate fires started at the Hilton. A waiter was later charged with starting the Hilton fires. He allegedly admitted igniting curtains accidentally with a marijuana cigarette and it was revealed that he had earlier worked at the Grand. But police ruled out arson as the cause of the MGM disaster.

Whatever the cause of the fires, public confidence in Las Vegas was undermined. Gambling revenues in the first three months of 1981 fell by more than $20 million as punters decided that the neon city was no longer such a safe bet. Many even questioned the whole idea of Las Vegas – brash, artificial and unashamedly money-oriented – and asked whether it had not become a faded monument to an earlier generation's vulgarity and bad taste.

But MGM had lost none of their enthusiasm for the Strip. On 30 July, 1981, the Grand re-opened after a $25 million rebuilding programme which included a $6 million computerised fire detection system. Each of the 2,900 rooms had four heat-activated sprinklers and a smoke detector, plus a ceiling speaker system to relay messages from the ground-floor emergency room, manned 24 hours a day. There a computer monitored 1,300 locations throughout the hotel, and could activate 1,000 different safety devices to halt the spread of fire and smoke, and guide guests to safety.

Corridors and stairways were all fitted with smoke detectors, plus an elaborate system of fans to isolate and remove fumes quickly. All doors could be opened automatically so no escape routes would be blocked. There were also manually triggered alarms on walls throughout the building. And guests booking in could put their minds at rest by watching a five-minute film, narrated by veteran Hollywood star Gene Kelly, on what to do in emergencies.

'People are very conscious of fire,' hotel president Rothkopf told newsmen. 'That is why we have spent all this money on equipment. This is now one of the safest high-rise hotels anywhere in the world.'

Mount St Helens Eruption (1980)

For years Mount St Helens volcano slumbered like a fairy-tale dragon, only occasionally rumbling and snorting. But at 8.32 a.m. on a sunny Sunday morning, 18 May 1980, its glistening snow-capped peak suddenly erupted with a cataclysmic blast that caused the mightiest volcanic landslide ever recorded.

The explosion which was equivalent to 500 Hiroshima atomic bombs was so powerful it was heard 200 miles away, and it was feared the climate of the entire world would be changed.

In the immediately surrounding area it turned 200 square miles of lush farmland, forests, streams and rivers near the Pacific coast of America's western state of Washington into an eerie grey, crater-strewn wilderness of death and devastation. Towns up to 100 miles away were paralysed by a blizzard of hot, choking gases and ash that plunged them into midnight blackness orchestrated with flashes of lightning and claps of thunder. Within days another massive ash cloud had circled the globe, miles high, causing hazy skies and strange sunsets all around the world.

Scientifically, the Mount St Helens disaster has been called the most spectacular and important geophysical event of 1980. In fact, it was probably the best-monitored and most vividly recorded major volcanic eruption in history – one that may well rival legendary Vesuvius in the telling in school classrooms for the rest of this century and beyond.

Incredibly, scientists had predicted for five years that the 9,677 feet volcano, called Fire Mountain in Red Indian language, was likely to erupt. But the U.S. Geological Survey team keeping watch could only estimate it would happen 'perhaps before the end of the century'. It had erupted only five times in 280 years. The last time had been 123 years earlier in 1857.

But on Thursday, 27 March 1980, the volcano, one of 15 in the Cascade range of mountains, suddenly started to boil up, sparking a series of events that amazed all the experts. They warned people that an explosion was now imminent and, but for that and the establishment of no-go areas for the public, the ultimate death toll of 60 would have been horrifically higher.

The volcano dominated a rugged landscape of peaks, fir forests and valleys with streams and rivers overflowing with salmon, trout, wild animals and birds, so it was a favourite haunt for thousands of campers, hitch-hikers and hunters. Around it were dotted logging camps, weekend homes and small towns and hamlets.

The authorities thought they had done all they could to minimise the risk of death and injury. The mountain itself was peppered with monitoring devices to give the earliest possible warning of the 'Big Bang'.

The area immediately around it was declared a red zone barred to everyone. And circling that was a larger blue zone supposed to be open only to people with special permits, such as geologists, official photographers, lawmen and approved officials.

So, with the time bomb already ticking, the scene was set. For seven weeks, throughout the rest of March and April to the middle of May, the volcano simmered, shuddered and hiccuped. It was as if the great, craggy monster was just turning over in its sleep, belching acrid fumes from its mouth.

Then came the first danger signs. A fracure nearly three miles long snaked across the summit and the north face began to bulge as thousands of tons of molten rock started to move inside the volcano. It swelled at a rate of about five feet a day until it stood out 320 feet like a grotesque boil on the beauty-spot mountain's neck.

Still, the watching scientists did not quite know what to expect. But by this time, as publicity had mounted nationwide, the public were throwing all caution to the wind and letting curiosity get the better of them. They flocked to the area from all over the country in the hope of seeing the eruption. And many were to pay for it with their lives. Sheriff Les Nelson, of nearby Cowlitz County, who helped police the blue no-go zone, said later: 'Loggers, tourists, property owners, newsmen and mountain climbers violated the rules constantly. They went over, under, around and through our blockades. Nobody would listen to us.'

Then, as breakfast sizzled in frying pans on that sun-kissed Sunday morning in May, the unbelievable happened. Geologist David Johnston, 30, was manning an observation post five miles north of St Helens sending reports back to the Government Geological Survey base. At 8.32 a.m. he radioed: 'Vancouver! Vancouver! This is it. The mountain's going.' And at that moment he died – blasted to eternity. His body was never found.

In split-second sequence there was first an earthquake reading magnitude five on the Richter scale, followed by an earth shattering explosion that caused the catastrophic avalanche. More than a mile of the north face, consisting of earth, snow and boulders of ice and rock, rocketed downwards. The intense heat of the blast melted the ice into an estimated 46 billion gallons of water.

That, in turn, created a 30-mile wide maelström of mudflow and flood that

MOUNT ST HELENS ERUPTION

Mount St Helens erupts, sending smoke, ash and ice chunks high into the air

cascaded 15 miles down the nearby North Toutle River and valley at speeds up to 80 miles an hour, obliterating everything in its path and burying it to depths of up to 150 feet. The avalanche was quickly overtaken by a 200 miles an hour, 20-mile wide horizontal hurricane of scalding ash, suffocating gasses and boulder-size débris that scythed down all that stood in its way for miles around.

More than 20 idyllic lakes and 150 miles of trout and salmon streams were destroyed. Thousands of fish were boiled alive in the sizzling waters. Others leapt spectacularly ashore to die on land. An estimated two million birds and animals were wiped out, including deer, elk, bears and goats.

Huge logging trucks and bulldozers were swept up and tossed about like confetti and about a million fir trees were flattened as the avalanche and blast clogged up the landscape with débris. Bridges snapped like twigs. Roads, railway lines and abandoned trains, buses and cars were all consumed. Hundreds of homes were either destroyed or badly damaged.

More than 2,000 people fled from the advancing morass. People in towns as far as 10 miles away had been thrown from their beds by the blast. Police ordered residents up to 35 miles away to get out – quick. Soon more than 5,000 terrified people were huddled in temporary shelters as police closed all roads within 50 miles and planes were banned from flying anywhere near the area.

Static electricity from the eruption sparked a huge forest fire that rapidly engulfed a timber forest three miles from St Helens, hampering rescue workers and fleeing survivors.

And, as all this was happening, there was a third phenomenon. A gigantic gush of sulphurous ash, stony fragments and molten rock, blasted vertically 13 miles high from the mountain. Blast after blast ripped the guts out of the volcano for nine hours, sending an estimated 400 million tons of débris into the earth's atmosphere and outer space.

The colossal cloud, blown east and south by strong winds, quickly brought towns in Idaho and Montana to a stop as tons of grey ash descended on them and clogged them up. That day it piled up four inches deep throughout Washington State and neighbouring Oregon.

Washington State police spokesman William Richards said: 'It's totally dark here. You can't see anywhere.' James Lanterman, a 60-year-old radio ham, broadcast dramatically from his mobile home 20 miles north-east of St Helens: 'The air is so full of smoke and pumice stone that a person wouldn't live outside. The falling dust is inches thick and the eruptions from the mountain are causing a terrific lightning storm.' The ash blanket was so enormous that some towns even sent out snowploughs to clear routes for emergency services. Hospitals filled up with people complaining of breathing problems. In Montana Governor Thomas Judge ordered all State offices, schools and businesses to close and urged people to stay indoors and breathe through gauze masks.

All road and rail services in Washington State were halted for hundreds of miles, and planes were cancelled and grounded as far away as Denver because of hazards to visibility and also to engines, posed by the dust. In fact, the mountain spewed more ash and rock than Vesuvius in A.D. 79.

Just two days after the blast the massive ash cloud had cast a shadow nearly 2,500 miles long and 1,000 miles wide across the U.S. It took only three days to cross the whole of America and only 17 to go right round the world. It shaded the sun and Dr. William Donn, of Columbia University's Geological Observatory, said he feared it would throw a shroud around the earth and cause average temperatures everywhere to drop by one degree.

As the dust settled on the disaster area, incredible tales of death, survival and heroism began to emerge. One victim was the pilot of a crop-dusting plane 100 miles from Mount St Helens who was killed when he flew into a power line – either because he was blinded by volcanic ash or because it got into his engine.

Fred Rollins, 58, and his wife, Margery, 52, tourists from California who had talked their way through the blue no-go zone blockade early on the fateful Sunday morning, were found dead in their car, buried by molten mud.

Rescue pilot Captain Robert J. Wead, one of the team of helicopter aces who, amazingly, managed to pluck 198 people from the jaws of the disaster, said: 'People were fried in the heat.'

Other dead included campers – a young father found with his arms around his two small sons, and a young couple in a tent, crushed by toppled trees.

But the most astonishing victim was 84-year-old Harry Truman. He had lived for 50 years in the shadow of Mount St Helens and had built himself a

Vesuvius erupts, again

Vesuvius, the Italian volcano that buried Pompeii and two other towns in AD 79, killing 2,000 people, gave the twentieth century a grim reminder of its power on 18 March 1944. She exploded in her most violent eruption for 40 years, and by the time she went quiet again eight days later, 26 people were dead, two villages were under lava 30 feet deep, 5,000 people were homeless, and 60 Allied planes were unable to take off to fight the Nazis because of falling stones.

Crocodile allies

More than 1,000 Japanese soldiers were trapped in swampland on an island in the Bay of Bengal and bombarded by British artillery through the night of 19 February 1945. But the British had an unlikely band of 'allies'. As darkness fell, an army of huge crocodiles, attracted by blood in the water, moved in, attacking both the living and the dead. No one knows how many Japanese fell victim to the crocodiles, but by morning only 20 of the original 1,000 troops were still alive.

---

guest house beside lovely Spirit Lake, just five miles from the peak. Before the disaster, he was urged repeatedly to move out just in case there was a major eruption. But he stubbornly refused, saying: 'I am part of the mountain, the mountain is part of me.'

His brave stand made him a national hero overnight. Fan mail poured into his home from all over the world. He stood his ground – and died in the first seconds of the catastrophe, buried by the avalanche. Since then he has become a folk hero with books and songs written about him.

Other courageous men died, too, including official geologists and photographers monitoring the mountain from the fringe of the red total exclusion zone.

And there were the survivors. Like two loggers who walked out of the devastated area with more than two-thirds of their bodies burned.

Perhaps most remarkable of all were the family who had been camping out in a tent when it was buried by ash. Michael and Lu Moore and their two children, including a three-month-old baby, scrambled clear, then hiked across the disaster area for a day and a night before they were spotted and rescued by a helicopter crew.

Mrs Moore, 31, said later: 'It was horrible. We had to climb over trees that had been felled by the shockwaves. The acid stench of the ash was everywhere and it was hard to breathe.'

After it was all over – with damage estimated at £1 billion – scientists went back to the top of the volcano and found it had literally blown its top. The eruption, which made it the most active explosive volcano on mainland America for 4,500 years, had lopped 1,313 feet of the mountain's height and left a yawning, fiery hole measuring about one mile by two miles where the lava cone had been. It continued to smoulder and have minor eruptions for months afterwards.

U.S. President Carter went to the scene four days after the disaster and saw the devastation from a helicopter. He said: 'There is no way to describe it. It's a horrible sight. I don't think there is anything like it in the world. The moon looks like a golf course compared to here. It will take decades to clean up the damage and volcanic ash that has covered thousands of square miles.' He immediately declared a Federal emergency to clear the way for Government aid.

Eleven days after the disaster, rescue worker Robert Wead said: 'The area looks like a nuclear wasteland. Trees and vegetation are laid out flat – singed, burned, steaming, sizzling.'

But nature and mankind eventually stepped in to bring new life to the ravaged region. The débris flow and floods created new lakes and streams. By the end of 1981, volcanic lilies, ferns and berries were starting to grow across the bleak, grey landscape. Work started on salvaging the millions of tons of torn-up trees scattered across the area like giant toothpicks – enough timber to build up to 100,000 new homes and plans were finalized to plant millions of new trees. Meanwhile, the dragon mountain that flashed its fiery breath around the world resumed its restless sleep – until the next time.

St Valentine's Day Fire (1981)

It was 2 a.m. and time for the last dance for disco-goers celebrating St Valentine's Day at the Stardust. The club was packed with 841 young people, mostly under 21, enjoying themselves at Dublin's most popular night-spot.

Top prizes in a disco-dance competition had just been carried off by elated winners, the bar was about to close and the disc-jockey was introducing one of the last hit records that would be played. From the corner of his eye, the DJ noticed two club stewards carrying fire extinguishers towards what appeared to be a smouldering curtain. He gave the matter little attention thinking perhaps that someone's tossed-away cigarette had started a minor fire. Seconds later, the cries of the dying filled the air . . .

Within moments, the entire hall in the heart of Dublin's Artane working-class suburb, was ablaze. The vast ceiling began to simply melt in the intense heat, raining white-hot droplets onto panic-stricken teenagers. The lights went out and youngsters were trampled underfoot in the blind stampede to escape the fireball which enveloped the Stardust.

Forty six were killed and 130 injured, some of them terribly, in the early hours of 14 February 1981, in the worst single disaster the shocked city of Dublin had ever seen. The inferno, which may have been the work of an arsonist, had shot out of control so quickly because the hall was, literally, a plastic palace. The chairs overlooking the dance floor were covered in red plastic and stuffed with polyurethane foam which gives off a lethal black smoke when lit and can raise room temperatures in a fire to 1,500 degrees farenheit in under half a minute. The ceiling, reduced to a molten mass, was covered by tiles, which seemed to 'explode' according to witnesses. Inflammable curtains were draped around the walls and all the tables were made of plywood with plastic tops.

The Stardust was a tinder-box, waiting for the fuse to be lit. Yet, only four months previously, it had been inspected for fire safety – and approved. A judicial inquiry followed the holocaust and experts are now looking towards much more stringent safety standards. That, of course, is scant consolation to the families of those who died or the ones still bearing the terrible scars from the nightmare that marked St Valentine's Day.

None of those who survived will ever forget the scenes as fire took hold of the Stardust. 'It was complete pandemonium' said Eamonn Quinn, 24. 'There were flames everywhere and the whole place seemed to go up in a matter of minutes. The only way out was through the exit doors. The toilet windows were barred because vandals kept breaking the glass.'

As a scrum of screaming youths pushed through the main doors and five fire exits, DJ Colin O'Brien witnessed the horror. He said: 'There was just total panic. People grabbed on to me when I was on the stage. The fire spread in a matter of a couple of minutes. People were grabbing me and asking me the way out. I was being pushed and pulled in every direction. I ended up behind the stage and was pushed into a ladies' loo. I found there was fresh air there and not much smoke. I stayed there for a couple of minutes. Eventually smoke came in and I tried to get out through the roof of the loo – but it was made of concrete. I went out of the door and felt my way by the walls until I reached the exit. I couldn't see where I was going.'

Artane's parish priest, Father McMahon, was called from his bed as firemen fought a desperate battle to contain the flames, often being hampered by blocked exits and a crowd of morbid sightseers which had gathered. Said Father McMahon: 'The first thing I saw was people trapped in the front part of the building where the flames had cornered them in a toilet. The firemen outside were trying to break through the window, but were having a terrible time getting through.'

Bravely, Father McMahon dashed inside the blazing, dark and smoke-filled Stardust to see if he could help those still trapped. 'The ceiling was gone,' he said, 'and just the girders were left. There were bodies lying all over the place. The people who were dead were in God's hands immediately. The people who really needed help were those outside who were going frantic trying to rescue their sisters or girlfriends. That was really gruelling.' Father McMahon administered the last rites to those who were dying and then helped carry other victims, some of whom were appallingly injured, to a fleet of waiting ambulances. Later, he visited survivors in hospital and said: 'Some were so shocked that they did not know who they were.'

Secretary Maureen Ashe, 22, said: 'The noise and the screams were awful. I will live with that sound for the rest of my life.' Another survivor, 18-year-old Pauline Brady added: 'I saw three girls with their hair ablaze. They were so shocked they did not know what they were doing. I doubt very much if any of them got out alive.' Doorman Michael Cavanagh, who at one stage tried to combat the raging flames with a fire extinguisher, recalled: 'It was pointless. The place was a sheer inferno. There was panic everywhere. It was terrible.'

On the morning of 15 February, a cold, miserable Sunday, the grim task of identifying the bodies began. Grief-stricken mothers and fathers were led

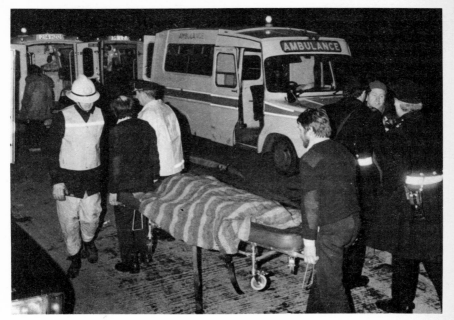

The dead and the injured are taken away by ambulance

around a makeshift morgue as officials and rescue workers started to piece together exactly who had died. In many cases, though, it was useless. So many bodies were burned beyond recognition that they were, eventually, only identified with the help of medical and dental records.

For the relatives of those who survived there was blessed relief. Yet in one heartbreaking and ironical case, a 46-year-old mother, Mrs Mary Coyne collapsed and died in the street after hearing that her son and two teenage daughters who had been at the disco were safe. For others, the scars of memory will remain for the rest of their lives.

A life, in John Keegan's case, without the two cherished daughters who perished in the fire. A third daughter, Antoinette, aged 20, survived. Mr Keegan found her after a frantic search of the city's hospitals and morgues. Her body was so badly charred that it seemed to be as black as coal. All remaining members of the Keegan family, including Antoinette, needed psychiatric help for many months after the blaze. The mental wounds of the 237 families affected were taking much, much longer to heal than any physical ones.

ST VALENTINE'S DAY FIRE

The day after the inferno, Irish premier Charles Haughey visited the charred shell of the Stardust and immediately announced an official day of mourning. He was told that some senior fire officers had been warning the Irish authorities 'for years' that there could be a major disaster at a discotheque. One, Mr Brian McMahon, a former chairman of Ireland's Chief Fire Officers' Association, told newsmen at the scene: 'I am not surprised that this terrible tragedy has occurred. I have given repeated warnings about the fire dangers in discotheques over the years. It is vital to have an inquiry into the whole area of fire inspection. Something is terribly wrong.' Prime Minister Haughey simply declared, on ordering a full public inquiry: 'Words cannot adequately express my sense of shock and anguish at this appalling disaster.'

He did, however, hear one heart-warming story to emerge from the tragedy – that of the courage of soldier Thomas Dowdall, who rescued at least four terrified teenage girls from the Stardust hall when the fire was raging at its peak. Seeing a barrel-shaped trolley full of empty bottles, which was apparently blocking an escape route, he dragged the screaming youngsters onto it and literally wheeled them to safety. One, 18-year-old Shirley McGregor, said later: 'He told me "I don't care if I break every bone in your body – you are going over the barrel." Without doubt he saved my life.'

Indeed, there were several acts of valour, although firemen later said that in some cases their own rescue efforts had been hampered. One senior fireman declared: 'It came almost to a fighting match to get people out of the way so we could go in to rescue those inside. I believe that some who were burned had gone back in to try to help their friends.'

In the aftermath of the Stardust disaster, a 200-page report prepared by the British Fire Research Centre at Borehamwood in Hertfordshire revealed that there was no single cause for the inferno, but a combination of several factors. All the material in the club, except for the ceiling tiles, was inflammable . . . something that building regulations in Britain and many other countries would never allow. Many of those who perished died from the poisonous fumes given off by these materials. Regulations to ban the use of such materials in Ireland had been under discussion in the country for a staggering four years. Ironically, they did come into effect . . . ten days after the Stardust disaster.

Allegations were made during the public inquiry that emergency exits at the Stardust had been locked – an accusation the management strenuously denied. Head doorman Thomas Keenan did say, however, that during certain periods on a disco-dance evening, exit doors were locked for up to 90 minutes at the start of the night in an effort to deter gatecrashers from slipping in without paying. Martin Donaghue, an electrical inspector, told the tribunal that he made 30 visits to the Stardust in 18 months to check instances of faulty lights.

Despite the assertions of one teenage girl witness that she saw two youths using a cigarette lighter to set fire to cloth-covered seats behind a curtained-off area of the dance hall, and the massive police hunt which followed, it has never been established whether there really was a mystery arsonist or arsonists.

However, there have been lessons learned from the Stardust disaster. Fire safety standards have been tightened and dance hall licences are closely scrutinized by city authorities, following the formation of a committee by members of the families of victims.

The parents are trying to persuade Dublin Corporation to build its own very first leisure centre in the city so that surviving children will have an alternative to other Stardusts. Ann Byrne, 22, who lost her 21-year-old brother Brian, in the blaze says: 'I've two children – and I don't want to watch them as teenagers walk into similar death traps.'

For the very real fear which still lingers, despite the political promises and the public inquiries, is that which Ann expresses along with so many other grieving relatives: it could so easily happen again.

The Potomac Airliner Crash (1982)

The storm had formed over New Orleans, swirling out of a trough of low pressure over the Gulf of Mexico. It swept north-east overnight, leaving the southern states under an unusually thick blanket of snow. In Alabama, a man died when the frozen branches of a tree fell on him. Atlanta, Georgia, and Chicago both recorded their lowest temperatures of the century. By the morning of Wednesday, 13 January 1982, the blizzards had reached the capital, Washington DC. At 1 p.m., the Federal Aviation Authority closed National Airport, a mile from the White House, for 73 minutes so ploughs could clear runways of a five-inch covering of snow.

In government offices all over the city, civil service chiefs anxiously scanned the cloud-laden skies, and soon after lunch, agreed to let all staff head for home early to beat the expected drifts. Soon all roads out of the capital were choked with cars inching their way cautiously through the blinding snow. A vast snake of traffic edged across the frozen River Potomac on the dual-carriageway 14th Street Bridge, part of Jefferson Davis Highway, the busiest route between Washington and the suburbs of Virginia. Then, at exactly 4 p.m., terror roared out of the sky in a disaster that was to claim 78 lives, and stun a nation.

Air Florida Flight 90 had been due to leave National Airport for Fort Lauderdale and Tampa at 2.15 p.m. But it was 3 p.m. before the 71 passengers – three of them carrying babies – left the departure lounge and filed into 21 rows of seats in their Boeing 737 twin-engined jet. Forty one seats were left empty. Captain Larry Wheaton, 35, and co-pilot Roger Pettit checked their instrument panels and apologised for yet more delays while airport workers de-iced the wings with glycol fluid. Though visibility was still restricted to less than half a mile, the airport had re-opened, and the two men watched an arriving plane taxi to the terminal, noting the huge icicles hanging from its wings.

'I'm certainly glad there's people taxiing on the same place I want to go' said Wheaton. 'I can't see the runway without these flags. Maybe further up . . .' Head stewardess Donna Adams looked out at the white landscape and said: 'I love it out here, look at all the tyre tracks in the snow.' Pettit was more concerned with practicalities. 'Boy, this is a losing battle, trying to de-ice those things,' he murmured, watching men at work on the wings. 'It gives you a false feeling of security, that's all it does.'

At 3.58 p.m. the Boeing finally taxied out for take-off from runway 36, at 6,870 feet the longest at the National. Passengers were relieved that their long wait was finally ending. The sun of Florida seemed even more inviting in this Arctic weather. The two pilots viewed the slushy runway through the still-falling snow, and elected to lift the nose wheel earlier than usual to help take-off. Just after 3.59 p.m. the plane left the ground.

Inside 30 seconds, the crew knew something was terribly wrong. 'God, look at that thing . . . that doesn't seem right,' said Pettit. 'Easy, vee-two, forward, forward,' urged Wheaton. 'Come on, forward . . . forward . . . just barely climb . . .' he continued. The plane was shuddering and shaking badly. A crewman yelled: 'Falling, we're falling.' Pettit turned to his captain: 'Larry, we're going down, Larry . . .' Wheaton replied coldly: 'I know it.' At 4.01 p.m. Flight 90 crashed.

On 14th Street Bridge, less than a mile from National Airport, drivers trapped in the crawling traffic jam heard the plummeting jet before they saw it. 'I heard a roar but I couldn't see anything for the snow,' said Justice Department clerk Lloyd Creger. 'The engines were so loud, they had to be going at full blast. I couldn't hear myself scream. Then I saw the plane coming out of the sky. It was just falling, but there didn't seem anything wrong with it. The nose was up, and the tail was down. Then there seemed to be no sound at all.' Another driver sobbed: 'I heard the noise of the jet getting louder and louder. I threw open my door and ran for my life. I didn't stop to turn round, I just heard a massive bang as the plane hit the bridge.'

The stricken plane only just cleared a railway bridge to the south of the two choked road spans. As it roared low over the helpless commuters, a wheel struck a truck on the southern carriageway, and the plane tumbled over the parapet into the Potomac between the road bridges. It ripped the tops off five cars, and swept others into the icy water.

Bridge collapses

Thirty five workers were killed on 15 October 1970, when a 400-foot span of a box-girder bridge being built over the River Yarra at Melbourne, Australia, buckled, twisted, and plunged on to a pier below, sparking oil blazes and oxy-acetylene explosions. The West Gate Bridge was to have been an eight-lane highway, two-and-a-quarter times as long as the Sydney Harbour Bridge. The Royal Commission of Inquiry into the disaster blamed: 'Mistakes, miscalculations, errors of judgement and sheer inefficiency.'

THE POTOMAC RIVER AIRLINER CRASH

The ice on the river shattered like a windshield hit by a rock, and débris bounced into the air. Stunned witnesses slowly realised the enormity of what had happened. 'There was twisted metal from crushed cars everywhere,' said reporter Al Rossiter. 'Some of the vehicles started burning, and the truck that had been hit was hanging over the edge at a 45 degree angle.' Vito Maggiolo said: 'There were bodies lying all over the bridge, and bodies on the ice in the river.' U.S. Air Force Sergeant Jerome Lancaster said: 'I counted about six or seven people in the water who were alive, but they were messed up. We threw a rope out to one passenger.'

The tail section of the Air Florida jet

Plane catches fire
All 301 people aboard died when a Saudi Arabian Tristar plane caught fire at Riyadh airport on 20 August 1980.

The Boeing had broken into three sections on impact. The nose plunged straight under the surface, killing everyone inside. The main fuselage belly-flopped and settled briefly, and horrified onlookers could see people inside, strapped to their seats, as the jagged wreckage slowly sank. But the tail miraculously floated for twenty minutes, and most of the survivors came from there. Five emerged, battered and shaken, and scuttled across the ice to safety. Others were spilled like dolls into the icy water, and desperately clung to pieces of wreckage or ice floes, screaming for help. People on the bridge threw every available cable out to them, and yelled: 'Hold on, help will be here soon.'

But the nightmare conditions – a city clogged by snow and traffic – made it impossible for the emergency services to react at full speed. Some staff were among those sent home early. Ambulances, fire-engines and police cars were trapped in the jams, having to swing on to the wide pavements in front of the White House to get through.

Incredibly, a second accident within minutes added to the chaos of the capital. A subway train packed with 1,000 commuters was derailed less than a mile and a quarter from the bridge, leaving three people dead, and many hurt. Emergency services had to be diverted to cope there, too.

The first rescue vehicles to reach 14th Street Bridge arrived on the Virginia side of the Potomac, at the same time as the first of a dozen police and Armed Forces helicopters arrived overhead, hovering dangerously close to the bridges to try to winch survivors to safety. And now the disaster took on almost bizarre proportions. TV crews alerted by the call-up of the emergency services arrived with their cameras, and began to send live coverage of the drama to a multi-million, coast-to-coast audience. Ameri-

---

Train plummets into river
A crowded train travelling between Samastipur and Banmukhi in the North India state of Bihar plunged off a bridge into the swollen River Bagmati on 6 June 1981, killing nearly 800 people in the world's worst-ever rail disaster.

Patricia Felch is rescued by a paramedic with the National Park Police

Inset: A U.S. Park Police helicopter hovers over a female passenger floating in the Potomac River

cans hardened by Hollywood disaster movies now watched with guilty fascination as real death and real heroism unfolded before their very eyes.

People were drowning and freezing to death less than 50 feet from the shore, in water where they could survive for only ten minutes. They feebly splashed around until the numbing cold paralysed muscles, making swimming impossible. They reached despairingly for lifelines hanging from helicopters, then slumped back beneath the surface, their hands too cold to keep a grip. A rescue official said: 'It was heartbreaking to see them so close and not be able to help. No one would live more than a few minutes in that water.'

Stewardess Kelly Duncan, 23, dressed only in her thin short-sleeved blouse and uniform skirt, failed repeatedly to grasp the rescue rings. It seemed she was doomed. Then helicopter pilot Donald Usher risked the lives of himself and crewman Gene Windsor by settling his craft almost on the water, while Windsor clambered out on to the landing skids, and snatched the helpless girl to safety. She was rushed to hospital with a broken leg and hypothermia – her temperature had fallen to 90F – but she survived, the only one of the five-strong crew to do so.

Priscilla Tirado was also in the water. She lunged at a cable but could not reach it. Her fading strength sent her under the surface, but she bobbed up again, and the helicopter crew threw her a lifebelt attached to a line. She pushed her arm through it, and seemed secure as the helicopter began to tow her to shore. But again she lost her grip, and plunged back into the water. Hundreds on the bridge and millions of telly-viewers watched her agony in despair. But one man reacted more positively.

Lennie Skutnik, a 38-year-old desk worker on his way home from the Congressional Budget Office, tore off his jacket and boots, and waded into the water, regardless of his own safety. Mrs Tirado, 23, was almost unconscious, but Skutnik managed to push, pull and even kick her to the bank, where willing hands dragged them ashore. They shared an ambulance to hospital, he suffering from hypothermia, she critically ill – and unaware that her husband Jose and two-month-old son Jason had both drowned.

Hero Skutnik, later praised by President Ronald Reagan, was modest about his part in the rescue. 'She just gave out,' he told reporters. 'Her eyes rolled back and she had just started to go under when I grabbed her. You could tell just by looking at her that she didn't have an ounce of energy left in her. She seemed to be losing the will to live. I didn't notice the cold at all while I was in the water. The only time I felt it was in the ambulance going to hospital afterwards. I noticed my toes were cold, that was all. I don't think I was any kind of hero. It was just an automatic reaction.'

Another hero did not live to tell his tale. Five times he grabbed lifelines thrown down by helicopters, but on every occasion he handed the rope to others who were dragged or lifted to shore. 'He could have gone first,' said pilot Donald Usher. 'We threw the ring to him but he passed it to a man who was bleeding badly from a head injury. We went back four times, and each time he kept passing the ring to someone else, including three ladies hanging on to the tail section. The last time we went back, he had gone. The ice had formed over where he had been. We stayed there ten minutes, just in the hopes he had crawled into the fuselage and found an air pocket, but it became obvious he had gone. He's the real hero of this whole thing. If you were in his situation, a hundred yards from shore and knowing that every minute you were closer to freezing to death, could you do it? I really don't think I could.'

Co-pilot Gene Windsor said: 'The guy was amazing, I've never seen such guts. It seemed to me he decided that the women and the injured man needed to get out of there before him, and even as he was going under he stuck to that decision. Afterwards we looked everywhere for him, but he was gone.' Only when all the bodies had been recovered was the identity of the bald man with the black moustache established. Arland Williams, 46, a federal government employee, was the only one who had died from drowning alone. All the rest had broken limbs.

Mercifully, most of the plane's passengers died instantly on impact. But some of the 78 victims died horrifyingly slowly. One elderly man's story was told by Salvation Army major Harold Anderson: 'He was alive when police saw him under the ice, and he watched rescuers trying to get to him to get him out of the water. He was trying frantically to get out, but by the time they got the ice broken he was gone. They couldn't revive him.'

The first survivors were admitted to the George Washington Medical Center 45 minutes after the crash. Three-and-a-half hours after the disaster hospitals were officially told to expect no more patients. Only five people aboard the plane had survived. Four drivers on the bridge had been killed. Sixteen people were in hospital.

The grisly search for bodies went on long after dark. Floodlights and the flashing lights of rescue vehicles lit up an eerie scene as men with boathooks

---

Death in Egypt

The world's worst single-vehicle death crash happened in Egypt on 9 August 1973. A bus crashed into an irrigation canal, killing 127 people.

THE POTOMAC RIVER AIRLINER CRASH

fished from a tug and rubber dinghies between the ice floes near the wreckage of the white and blue Air Florida jet. Helicopters switched their attention from the river to the bank, airlifting the less seriously hurt away from the tragic scene. Bodies were laid out in the snow, and a makeshift mortuary set up in a tent. Army ice-breakers arrived, and divers in specially thick wetsuits tried to batter their way into the fuselage, to reach bodies still strapped into seats. At dawn, rescue teams were greeted by the heartbreaking sight of a woman and a baby floating, frozen stiff on the icy surface.

Two people are hauled away from the jetliner wreckage

The world's worst famine

More than 20,000,000 died from famine in northern China between 1969 and 1971, it was revealed in May 1981. One hundred years earlier, 9,500,000 peasants had died in a famine in the same area.

Diving operations continued over the next week, but it was a slow process. Visibility under water was reduced to 18 inches, and the jagged wreckage was surrounded by treacherous currents and submerged ice. Spilled aviation fuel made the wreckage slippery, and the Arctic weather never let up. One diver had to be rescued when his breathing valve froze up, and a barge carrying a crane was holed by ice. Divers were restricted to 30 minutes at a time in the 25 feet deep water, despite maximum protective clothing. It took them seven days to recover the 'black box' flight recorders, vital to the subsequent inquiry into why the crash happened.

Because of the snow, no-one, not even the control tower staff at National Airport, had seen Flight 90 leave the ground. The Federal Aviation Authority investigators had to rely on the automatic tapes of the pilots, quoted earlier, and the evidence of the few survivors.

Both stewardess Kelly Duncan and passenger Burt Hamilton, 40, spoke of the plane shuddering badly soon after lift-off. Mr Hamilton, whose seat was by the galley at the back of the jet, said: 'I knew something was wrong as it took off. The plane seemed to take an awful long time to pick up speed. It really started vibrating – a strong shaking, so bad that I tightened my seat belt and started to pray a lot.'

Businessman Joseph Stiley, 42, a private pilot, also claimed he knew that all was not well. Thumbing through his papers with his secretary Patricia

Mysterious meteorite

At precisely 7.17 a.m. on 30 June 1908, a mighty meteorite or some other mysterious object exploded over the Tunguska River valley in northern Siberia causing the most terrible devastation. Two thousand square miles of forest were laid bare. Herds of reindeer were incinerated. Nomads 45 miles away were hurled to the ground and their tents torn away. The explosion was heard 600 miles away. Yet even today no one knows the cause nor the death toll of a blast equivalent to that of a 30-megaton nuclear bomb.

Felch, he turned to her as the engines roared and said: 'We're not going to make it, we're going down.' Later, in hospital with two fractured legs, he said: 'Things were not going right soon after we started down the runway. We didn't have the speed. It seemed like the pilot tried to abort, but ran out of runway. He had to make the decision to go, so we took off. We got up a little bit, but it didn't climb like a normal 737. We got a fairly decent angle, then stalled and we went down. We were in the air only 20 or 30 seconds before impact, when I passed out.'

The disaster was the first major crash since President Reagan had fired 11,500 striking air traffic controllers the previous August. The controllers' union had warned then that pilots flying blind in winter would miss the help from the ground they usually relied on, but Federal Aviation chiefs dismissed air traffic control error as a possible cause of the accident.

The crash also raised questions about the safety of National, rated by pilots as one of the trickiest airports in America. Though accident-free since 1949, the airport – maintained by the government mainly for the convenience of Congressmen and civil servants – is set in the heart of a heavily built-up urban area, and can be used only by smaller jets. Larger aircraft have to fly out of Dulles Airport, 30 miles west of the capital. The short runways at National leave no room for second thoughts by pilots, and flight-paths are awkward, partly because of minimum noise requirements, partly because planes taking off have to make a sharp left-hand turn to avoid the 555-foot high Washington Monument.

But investigators were concerned not with the National's shortcomings, but with why Flight 90 hit 14th Street Bridge when it should have been at least 500 feet above it. They concentrated on three possibilities: fuel contamination causing loss of power, pilot error, and the most likely cause of the crash, ice.

Since man first took to the air, ice on the wings, restricting their power to lift, or ice in the engine, distorting air intake and reducing power, have

---

Ships collide

Fifty lives and £2,500,000 worth of ships were lost because of fog in the English Channel on the night of 11 January 1971. The Panamanian tanker *Texaco Caribbean* collided with a freighter nine miles off Folkestone, split in two and sank with eight crew. Next night 21 more sailors died when the German freighter *Brandenberg* struck the wreckage. And a month later the Greek freighter *Niki* went down with 21 hands after also hitting wreckage.

always been a danger. And within days of the Potomac disaster, it was revealed that, just one week before the crash, the British Civil Aviation Authority had warned their American counterparts that the Boeing 737, normally one of the world's safest aircraft, was particularly vulnerable to icy conditions. The British Airline Pilots' Association had reported that the jets tended to pitch up or roll unaccountably when ice was on the wings. And BALPA's technical secretary, Terence Staples, said: 'There does not have to be a large deposit. Even a small amount, which might not be easy to see, can cause difficulties.'

Boeing immediately instructed all airlines to ensure that the wings of 737 jets were inspected before take-off, and any ice removed. And the British authorities ordered 737 pilots to increase take-off speeds by up to five knots, and to slow the rate at which they allowed the nose to rise.

The Australian Bushfires (1983)

Even by the dusky, throat parching standards of Southern Australia it had been a scorcher of a summer. In the big cities of Adelaide and Melbourne everyone who could headed for the Great Ocean Road and resorts like Airey's Inlet in the hope of a cool dip and a brief respite from the sweltering heat.

For weeks now fire chiefs had been repeating their warnings of a tinderbox death trap. In some parts of the Outback there had been no rain for three years or more. But it was the Bush – the scrub and grassland lying between the major towns and cities and the actual Outback – that was threatened by a single spark. For the thousands of Bush dwellers, many of them third and fourth generation families, it was a risk they were prepared to live with. The true Bush townships of 200 and 300 inhabitants live a tranquil existence, their arid soil turned into rich pasture by irrigation, time and toil.

From the moment they enter school children learn firefighting techniques and by their teens are willing recruits to their local 'Bush Brigade', carrying water packs with powerful hand pumps on them to deal with any sudden outbreaks. The moment a fire breaks out the village fire truck, klaxon sounding, rounds up a platoon of volunteers. Dozens more 'beaters', the name given to huge spade-like mops, are deployed in the damping down operation.

Huge fines, and even jail, are the penalty for careless tourists who throw a match from a car window or dump a bottle that could magnify the sun's rays to ignition point.

The dangers were well enough broadcast, well enough understood. But awareness was not enough to prevent the Travelling Inferno that swept across Victoria and South Australia faster than an express train. Shortly after 3.30 p.m. on 16 February 1983, ironically Ash Wednesday in the ecclesiastical calendar, the first alarm was raised.

The first fires started in the Dandenong Ranges where temperatures had nudged past the 110 degrees mark on the hottest February day on record. There were to be conflicting theories as to the cause. Arson was suspected in several instances, and there was the possibility of overhead power cables snapping in the unusually strong 50 mph winds and setting light to the eucalyptus trees. But one fact could not be disputed. When the fires began there was simply no controlling them.

Anyone who has ever suffered from a bad cough will have reached for the menthol and eucalyptus medicine resting on many a medicine cabinet shelf. Without the menthol, eucalyptus is a killer not a cure. The oil filled leaves of the eucalyptus tree are highly inflammable. The bark burns with the speed of paper, the foilage erupting in a fireball. As if bowled along the ground by a mighty hand the fireballs gather speed, moving at speeds of more than 70 mph. Ash Wednesday's blazes began simultaneously in no less than seven places, three outside Adelaide in South Australia, four within 50 miles of Melbourne in the state of Victoria. Soon they were moving along fronts of up to 100 miles with murderous intent. Death and destruction followed.

Cockatoo, a tiny town east of Melbourne was the first township to be engulfed in the holocaust. By now the 40 foot high fireballs, fed by the occasional wood-framed house, were capable of leaping 50 feet into the air and vaulting a six lane highway. A survivor was to describe later how he watched from his verandah the evil golden globes sweeping across a ridge 500 yards away and five minutes later engulfing the home from which he and his family managed to escape.

A university expert was later to describe the bush fire that swept through Cockatoo as '30 times more intense' than normal. The County Fire

Fire at the Club Cinq-Sept

On Saturday, 1 November 1970, the popular Club Cinq-Sept was packed with young French people not only from the small town of St Laurent de Pont, but also Grenoble, Aix-les-Bains and Chambery. The interior of the club was trendily decorated with plastic psychedelic structures creating a grotto-like effect. To prevent gatecrashers, all exits, apart from the main turnstile, were locked on this particular night. At around 1.40am a boy dropped a match onto a cushion. Within one minute the entire psychedelic interior of the club was a fury of flames, fumes and dripping plastics. Only 30 people managed to escape through the main turnstile before it was jammed with bodies. The fact that there was not even a telephone on the club's premises meant a considerable delay until the fire brigade arrived, by which time nothing could be done. One hundred and forty six youngsters died in France's worst ever fire.

Obviously, safety and building regulations had been ignored, and the Mayor, two building contractors and the surviving owner were given suspended sentences, although many parents felt these were too lenient.

Two of the
8500 homeless
survivors of
Australia's Ash
Wednesday
bush-fires.

THE AUSTRALIAN BUSH FIRES

Aberfan Landslide

On 21 October, 1966 a rain-sodden, 800-foot-high tower of waste coal slag slipped, tumbling half a mile before slowing down. In its path it engulfed a school, a row of cottages and a farm. In the school the children were attending morning service on the final morning before their half-term holidays. The death toll was 116 children and 28 adults; hardly any family in the small community did not suffer a bereavement. Worst of all, the question of the tip's safety had been raised many times, and the danger signs had been totally ignored.

Authority had not time to muster sufficient water tankers to fight the fireballs. There was a call to evacuate. And then the flames hit Cockatoo.

With one road in and one road out there was nowhere to run. People hid in their homes, under their homes. They tried to escape by car, but in more than one case the Travelling Inferno, now moving at speeds of up to 100 mph overtook them and engulfed them. In the hills outside Cockatoo a terrified family of eight hid inside a water tank for 10 hours as the fire raged outside and the water inside almost boiled. But the greatest act of survival was to be inside the village school whose brick walls at least withstood the flames. There 120 children cowered under wet blankets as their parents played hosepipes on the roof. By daybreak on Thursday 29 people had lost their lives and more than half the town's houses were just blackened stumps. As relief helicopters hovered overhead Cockatoo resembled a war zone. But the death toll was to increase as the angry flames turned their attentions elsewhere.

At Mount Gambier in South Australia a family of five died in another car horror as they tried to race the flames to safety. Twelve firemen found their two water tankers as much use as covered wagons against the Sioux nation. They, too, died.

To the West of Melbourne the holiday hamlet of Aireys Inlet was wiped off the face of the seared earth. Holidaymakers wept openly on the beach as kangaroos jumped from clifftops into the sea and drowned as they too tried to escape.

Trapped between the Bush and the Ocean people staying in their beach homes at Lorne and Angleseay had spent a bizarre and horrifying Wednesday night vigil on the sands as the fire ravaged their homes on the clifftops above.

In the heart of Melbourne startled residents could now see the smoke on ridges less than 20 miles away. They could taste the ash on their tongues and the rank, acrid smell that follows a firestorm filled their nostrils. They could taste something else too; the fear that they might be next.

Ever since the first raising of the alarm on the Wednesday afternoon the Victoria County Fire Authority, swelled by hundreds of volunteers, had worked tirelessly round the clock. In one forest blaze alone, near Warburton 700 fire-fighters with 50 water tankers, stood their ground. Nearer Melbourne bulldozers and excavators stood ready to dig huge fire troughs in which, hopefully, the flames would simply die away.

Spotter planes with infra-red equipment added a technological touch to the grim scenario. By Friday morning the fires were largely under control. But the dangers of further outbreaks were said by the Victoria County Fire Chief to be 'perilously high'.

Acrimony and recrimnation entered the arena. The Prime Minister Malcolm Fraser abandoned his general election campaign to deal with the disaster. He ordered massive federal aid to help the homeless and ordered a weekend of national mourning. Forty eight hours of holocaust horror had seen Australia's worst ever bush fire claim the lives of more than 70 people.

It had rendered more than 8,500 people homeless, had devastated some 150,000 acres of farm and forest land, crippling the dairy industry and bankrupting the fruit growers.

More than 200,000 sheep and cattle had perished. No one could count the

Fire in Sao Paulo

On 1 February, 1974 fire broke out on the eleventh floor of an office skyscraper called the Joelma Building in Sao Paulo, Brazil. Probably ignited in an overheated air-conditioning vent, the fire spread with horrifying speed because the interior of the building was constructed in highly-inflammable materials. Within minutes 650 people were cut off by the flames. Several people were trampled to death in the initial panic, as they fled to the upper floors. However, the flames quickly spread upwards and the only escape was to jump to almost certain death. Despite heroic efforts by the fire services, their ladders were not long enough. Ropes were thrown from helicopters to haul people from the roof before the heat died down enough for them to land. The fire was brought under control after four hours, by which time 220 people had died, indirectly because of Sao Paulo's inadequate building regulations and undermanned fire-fighting services.

THE AUSTRALIAN BUSH FIRES

> The Black Hills of Dakota were in mourning in 1972 after 14 inches of rain, the normal average for a year, fell in just one night. The disaster began late on Friday, 9 June. The downpour ran off the hills in a torrential flood, funneled through narrow canyons, until it washed over an earth dam and sent a five-foot high wall of debris-filled water through the heart of Rapid City, the second largest town in South Dakota. By the time the flood subsided on Saturday morning, 237 people were dead, five were missing and 5,000 were homeless in a 30-mile long, half-mile wide path of sudden destruction.

numbers of dead among the protected species of kangaroo and koala bear. An early estimate of the damage put the figure at £500 million.

The soul searchers asked themselves: 'What went wrong? Where did the fire-fighting system break down?' But there was no simple answer, except to blame the weather. In 1939 71 people had died in bush fires in Victoria on a day known nationally as 'Black Friday'. Now February 16th 1983 has taken its place in the calendar of catastrophes. For the people of Southern Australia, Ash Wednesday is a day they will never forget.